1/09

639.34
Skomal

D1008615

Freshwater Aquarium

2nd Edition

Gregory Skomal

Howell
Book House™

Copyright © 2005 by Wiley Publishing, Inc., Hoboken, New Jersey. All rights reserved.
Photos copyright © Aaron Norman.

Howell Book House
Published by Wiley Publishing, Inc., Hoboken, New Jersey

For general information on our other products and services or to obtain technical support please contact our Customer Care Department within the U.S. at (800) 762-2974, outside the U.S. at (317) 572-3993 or fax (317) 572-4002.

Wiley also publishes its books in a variety of electronic formats. Some content that appears in print may not be available in electronic books. For more information about Wiley products, please visit our web site at www.wiley.com.

Library of Congress Cataloging-in-Publication Data:

Skomal, Gregory.
   Freshwater aquarium/Gregory Skomal.-- 2nd ed.
      p. cm. -- (Your happy healthy pet)
   Includes index.
   ISBN-10: 0-7645-8377-8 (cloth)
   ISBN-13: 978-0-7645-8377-3
  1. Aquariums.   I. Title.   II. Series.
   SF457.S53 2005
   639.34--dc22

                                 2005002069

Printed in the United States of America

10 9 8 7 6 5 4 3

2nd Edition

Book design by Melissa Auciello-Brogan
Cover design by Michael J. Freeland
Book production by Wiley Publishing, Inc. Composition Services

About the Author

Gregory Skomal is an accomplished marine biologist, underwater explorer, photographer, aquarist, and author. He has been a fisheries biologist with the Massachusetts Division of Marine Fisheries since 1987 and currently heads up the Massachusetts Shark Research Program. He has written numerous scientific research papers and has appeared in a number of film and television shark documentaries, including programs for National Geographic, Discovery Channel, ESPN, and CBS.

Although his research passion for the last twenty years has been sharks, he is also an avid aquarist and has written seven books on aquarium keeping. His home and laboratory are on the island of Martha's Vineyard off the coast of Massachusetts.

About Howell Book House

Since 1961, Howell Book House has been America's premier publisher of pet books. We're dedicated to companion animals and the people who love them, and our books reflect that commitment. Our stable of authors—training experts, veterinarians, breeders, and other authorities—is second to none. And we've won more Maxwell Awards from the Dog Writers Association of America than any other publisher.

As we head toward the half-century mark, we're more committed than ever to providing new and innovative books, along with the classics our readers have grown to love. This year, we're launching several exciting new initiatives, including redesigning the Howell Book House logo and revamping our biggest pet series, Your Happy Healthy Pet™, with bold new covers and updated content. From bringing home a new puppy to competing in advanced equestrian events, Howell has the titles that keep animal lovers coming back again and again.

Contents

Shopping List

You'll need to do a bit of stocking up before you bring your fish home. Below is a basic list of some must-have supplies. For more detailed information on the selection of each item below, consult chapter 2. For specific guidance on what fish food you'll need, review chapter 6.

- ☐ Tank
- ☐ Tank stand
- ☐ Hood
- ☐ Filter
- ☐ Water quality test kit
- ☐ Air pump
- ☐ Airstones
- ☐ Air hose
- ☐ Heater
- ☐ Thermometer

- ☐ Aquarium light
- ☐ Gravel
- ☐ Plants
- ☐ Algal cleaner
- ☐ Aquarium vacuum
- ☐ Fishnet
- ☐ 5-gallon bucket
- ☐ Siphon hose
- ☐ Fish food

There are likely to be a few other items that you're dying to pick up before bringing your fish home. Use the following blanks to note any additional items you'll be shopping for.

- ☐ _____
- ☐ _____
- ☐ _____
- ☐ _____
- ☐ _____
- ☐ _____
- ☐ _____
- ☐ _____

Pet Sitter's Guide

We can be reached at (___)_____-_____ Cellphone (___)_____-_____

_____

We will return on _____ (date) at _____ (approximate time)

Fish species _____

_____

_____

Other individual to contact in case of emergency _____

_____

Care Instructions

In the following three blanks let the sitter know what to feed, how much, and when; what tasks need to be performed daily; and what weekly tasks they'll be responsible for.

Morning_____

_____

_____

_____

Evening _____

_____

_____

_____

Other tasks and special instructions _____

_____

_____

_____

Part I

Getting Started

The Freshwater Fish

Eye

Nostril

Mouth

Gill Cover

Pectoral Fin

Scale

Dorsal Fin

Pelvic (Ventral) Fin

Anal Fin

Lateral Line

Caudal (Tail) Fin

Chapter 1

About Freshwater Fish

Y ou are reading this book because of your interest in owning and maintaining an aquarium. So you are likely a fish enthusiast, like me. The world of fish is both fascinating and complex. This book will help you to understand this watery world and teach you what you need to know to successfully set up and maintain a freshwater aquarium.

Of course, before you get started you should have a general knowledge of fish, their anatomy and biology, as well as a thorough understanding of their proper care and husbandry. First, let's take a look at fish anatomy and what makes these animals unique. Then we'll examine the aquarium and the importance of meeting the biological needs of fish.

Fish Evolution

The group of aquatic animals that we call fish has evolved over 400 million years to be the most numerous and diverse of the major vertebrate groups (animals with backbones). Fishes have permeated all the waters of the world, adapting with an incredible variety of forms, lifestyles, and behaviors. From seasonal freshwater streams, desert springs, and salty bays to coral reefs and the deep abyss, different species of fish have found and created niches for themselves.

Fish Terminology

Many folks think that the plural of fish is "fish," but actually when you are referring to more than one kind or species of fish, the plural of fish is "fishes." For example, there are many kinds of fishes in the ocean. However, more than one fish of the same species is fish, as in, "These Guppies are beautiful fish." And it's also "fish" when you are talking generally about the fish as a particular type of animal.

There are well over 20,000 known species of fish that currently inhabit the earth, and many are discovered every year.

Since salt water covers more than 70 percent of the earth's surface and fresh water only 1 percent, one would expect that there would be many more marine (saltwater) species than freshwater species of fishes. Actually, 41 percent of the world's fishes inhabit strictly fresh water. Although quite similar in many ways to their marine counterparts, freshwater fish have adapted to a much wider range of habitats and a greater variety of water conditions. Hence, freshwater fish are typically hardier than their marine friends and much easier to maintain. That's good for you.

Fish Biology

Because there are no fewer than 8,000 species of freshwater fish, it is difficult to describe the "typical" fish. However, all fish have some common characteristics. Since water is 800 times denser than air, fish have developed a variety of ways to move easily, breathe, and feed in this dense medium. The biological adaptations for life in a watery world include the body shape, fins, scales, and swim bladder.

Body Shape

A great deal can be learned about a species of fish by looking at its body form or shape. Fish that are streamlined or bullet-shaped, like Neon Tetras, are well

Streamlined fish, like this Malawi Golden Chichlid, are adapted to the open waters of lakes and ponds.

adapted to the open waters of freshwater lakes and ponds. On the other hand, flat or stocky fish, like Catfish, typically live on or close to the bottom.

Fins

All species of fish have fins in one form or another. The fins are critically important appendages that enable the fish to propel, stabilize, maneuver, and stop itself. In some cases, fins have developed to protect the fish as well. Again, depending on the type of fish and the habitat it lives in, the fins can take on many shapes and functions. Bottom, sedentary, or slower moving fish typically have rounded fins, while faster, open water fish generally have longer, pointed fins.

Fish fins are either paired or unpaired. The only fins that come in pairs are the pectoral and pelvic fins, while the dorsal, anal, and caudal fins are unpaired. The pectoral fins are the paired fins closest to the head. The fish uses these fins to stabilize, turn, maneuver, hover, and swim backwards. These fins are generally found just behind or below the gills on each side of the fish, under the midline of the body.

The pelvic fins are also paired and vary the most in position. In some fish, they lie under the fish toward the rear. In others, such as many tropical species, the pelvics are closer to the head under the pectorals. In general, the pelvic fins act as brakes while aiding in stabilizing and turning the fish.

The dorsal and anal fins are unpaired fins that are found protruding from the top and bottom of the fish, respectively. Dorsal fins may be elongated or short, elaborate or simple, singular or multiple. In some species of fish, the dorsal or anal fin may be completely lacking. Both fins help stabilize the fish and keep it moving straight.

The caudal or tail fin is a single fin largely responsible for propelling the fish forward. This fin can also assist in turning and braking. Faster fish have deeply forked caudal fins, while many deep-bodied and bottom fish have square or rounded tail fins.

In general, the main supporting structures of fish fins are soft rays. However, anyone who has handled a fish knows that the dorsal, anal, pectoral, or pelvic fins of many species also have spines. These sharp, bony structures provide protection against predators and can certainly hurt us as well.

Scales

The bodies of most tropical fish are covered with scales. The scales are composed of a hard bony substance and serve to protect the fish, reducing the chance of injury and infection. Covering the scales is a very thin layer of epidermal (skin)

The colors of this Discus depend on what type of pigment cells it has in its scales.

Fish Anatomy

There are thousands of different species of fishes, all uniquely adapted to their particular environments. However, most share fundamental characteristics that allow them to be classified together as fish.

Gills: These blood-filled structures enable the fish to absorb oxygen from the water in exchange for carbon dioxide.

Fins: These move the fish through the water, providing propulsion and steering.

Swim bladder: This organ fills up with air, thereby controlling the fish's level in the water column.

Lateral line: This sensory organ runs along the body and alerts the fish to movement close by, and also helps fish in schools to move in synchronization.

Scales: These streamline and protect the body of the fish as it moves through the water.

tissue that contains mucous cells. These cells produce the slime that we normally attribute to fish. The mucous coating not only protects the fish against injury and infection, but also helps the fish to swim more easily in the water, reducing friction between the body and the water.

The scales of a fish are actually translucent, like glass, and lack color. The vibrant colors of tropical fish come from specialized pigment cells called *chromatophores* in the deeper dermal layer of the skin. Fish that are clear, like the Glassfish, lack these pigment cells. The color of the fish depends on the types of chromatophores present. There are generally three types of chromatophores in fish: melanophores give fish the darker colors of black, brown and blue; xanthophores produce red, yellow, and orange; and iridophores reflect light, producing a silvery shine common to many fish.

Swim Bladder

As mentioned earlier, living in the dense medium of water presents a few problems for fish, and one of these is buoyancy. Maintaining a certain level in the

These Goldfish have a two-chambered swim bladder.

water column without having to expend a lot of energy is very important to fish. Therefore, most species have a special organ called the swim bladder. This gas-filled sac, located in the abdominal cavity of the fish, acts as a life vest, keeping the fish at the correct level in the water column.

There are many types of swim bladders. The Trout has a simple single-chambered sac, the Goldfish a two-chambered type, and the Angelfish a three-chambered bladder. Different species also use different methods to fill the swim bladder with air. Some have a direct connection between the esophagus and the bladder and simply swallow air to fill it. Others must rely on gas exchange from specialized blood vessels in the circulatory system to fill the swim bladder.

In addition to its role in buoyancy control, the swim bladder helps to mechanically amplify sound for better hearing in certain species of fish.

Feeding

Just as a fish's body shape can tell you a lot about its swimming habits, its mouth can tell you something about its feeding habits. Bottom feeders have downward pointing mouths, while surface feeders have mouths that point upward. For most fish, the mouth is at the end of the snout.

The size of the mouth is usually directly related to the size of the fish's preferred food. For example, large predatory fish like Oscars have larger oval mouths for consuming smaller fish. Fish that normally feed on small aquatic invertebrates, like Neon Tetras, have smaller mouths. Some tropical freshwater fish have specialized mouths for specialized feeding strategies. Plecostomus fish, for example, have special sucking mouths for bottom feeding.

Freshwater tropical fish have a relatively straightforward digestive system, which varies from species to species. In general, food passes from the mouth, down the esophagus, to the stomach, and through the intestine; wastes are expelled from the anal vent. However, several species lack true stomachs and instead have elongated, super-coiled intestines.

Breathing

Among the most primary of the basic needs of fish is oxygen. Like land animals, fish require oxygen to live. However, fish must derive oxygen from water and special respiratory organs, called *gills,* enable them to do so. The gills of a fish are analogous to our lungs: They supply oxygen and remove carbon dioxide from the blood of the fish. Then, oxygen is transported by the blood to the tissues where it is used to produce energy.

Most fish have four gills on each side of the head, protected by a single gill flap, or *operculum.* When a fish breathes, water is taken into the mouth and passed over the gills and out the operculum. As water passes over the membranes and filaments of the gills, oxygen is removed and carbon dioxide is excreted. To accomplish this, the gills have a very high number of blood vessels that deliver the oxygen to the rest of the fish via the blood.

Oxygen and carbon dioxide are not the only substances exchanged by the gills. Large amounts of ammonia are also excreted by the gills and, as you will see in chapters 2 and 3, ammonia is something that you have to be concerned with in the home aquarium.

Most fish have four gills on each side of the head, protected by a single gill flap. These are Butterfly Dwarf Cichlids.

The Fish's Senses

With few exceptions, fish have five senses that they use to feed, avoid predators, communicate, and reproduce.

The eyes of most fish are similar to our own, except they lack eyelids and their irises work much more slowly. Rapid changes in light intensity tend to shock a fish, a fact that should be taken into account by the aquarist. Gradual changes in light allow the fish to accommodate and avoid temporary blindness. The location of the spherical lenses of fish eyes renders most fish near-sighted. Although it varies from species to species, fish can detect color.

Hearing is an important part of a fish's life. Most fish do not posses external ears, but have an inner ear structure that is not noticeable on the outside of the fish. The auditory component of the inner ear consists of the *sacculus* and the *lagena,* which house the sensory components of hearing, the *otoliths.* Sound vibrations pass through the water, through the fish, and cause the otoliths in the inner ear to vibrate. In some cases the swim bladder articulates with the ear to amplify sound.

For fish, smell is particularly important in prey and mate detection. A fish has external nasal passages called *nares* that

In addition to the anatomical features already noted, fish typically possess other unique circulatory, digestive, respiratory, and nervous system features. Curious fishkeepers should examine the books listed in the appendix for more detailed descriptions of the unique anatomy of fish.

Freshwater and Saltwater Fish

As the name implies, salt water contains much higher concentrations of dissolved salt (sodium chloride) than fresh water. Although salt is the major constituent, there are many other dissolved elements in higher concentrations than allow water to pass into and out of the olfactory organ located above its mouth and below its eyes. Water flows through the nares and into the olfactory pits, where odors are perceived and communicated to the brain via a large nerve. The olfactory system of the fish is not attached to the respiratory system, as it is in humans, but remains isolated from the mouth and gills.

Taste is generally a close-range sense in fish and is especially helpful in identifying both food and noxious substances. In addition to being in the mouth, the taste buds are located on several external surfaces, such as the skin, lips, and fins. Catfish have specialized barbels with taste buds that help them detect food items in murky waters.

Fish have special organs comprising the lateral line system that enable them to detect water movements. Sensory receptors lying along the surface of the fish's body in low pits or grooves detect water displacement. The lateral line is easily visible along the sides of most fish. This unique system helps the fish detect other fish and avoid obstacles.

are found in fresh water. The amount of these dissolved "salts" in water is referred to as its *salinity* or *specific gravity*.

Although, anatomically, freshwater and saltwater fish are similar in appearance, they have evolved two very different ways of living in these chemically different environments. As a means of maintaining their internal salinity, freshwater fish drink very little water and produce large quantities of dilute urine. On the other hand, most marine fish drink large quantities of water and eliminate salts in small amounts of highly concentrated urine and feces, as well as at the gills. So the kidneys of these groups are very different.

An ancient interest in ornamental Goldfish led the Chinese to develop varieties with unusual characteristics.

Fish in Captivity

It is no surprise that humans have favored keeping fish in captivity for centuries. The Chinese kept the common Goldfish as far back as the year 265. Care and husbandry of fish has come a long way over the centuries, and in recent years there has been an incredible explosion in fish culture.

There was a time when most tropical freshwater fish kept in captivity were taken from their native habitats. This practice contributed to the degradation of tropical habitats and the local depletion of many species. Fortunately, modern husbandry techniques have taken the tremendous pressure off natural stocks; now, many of the common aquarium species are bred in captivity. Selective breeding has also allowed for the rearing of hardier fish that more easily adapt to the varying water conditions of the aquarium.

Your Responsibilities

Fish in their natural environment are subjected to many challenges. Most of these involve natural processes of predation, feeding, reproduction, and disease. Natural catastrophic events that alter water quality are rare, and fish can generally avoid them by swimming to other areas.

The Fishkeeper's Responsibilities

The fishkeeper (that's you) has an obligation to care for the fish that they have brought home. Because the fish are contained in an artificial environment, it is up to you to establish and to maintain their living space in an appropriate manner. The fishkeeper is responsible for providing:

- High water quality
- Proper feeding
- Correct water temperature
- A balanced fish community of the proper density
- Appropriate habitat and shelter
- Sufficient lighting

Make sure you are ready to accept these responsibilities and the daily chores that go with them before you start setting up your aquarium.

Fish in their natural habitats are usually very much responsible for their own well-being—when they are hungry, they seek out food; when the environment becomes hostile, they move to an area that is more hospitable. (A possible exception to this would be fish living in areas assaulted by man-made pollution.)

Fish maintained in an artificial environment are also faced with survival challenges. However, in the confines of the aquarium, most of these challenges cannot be met by the fish and must instead be met by the fishkeeper. When you take it upon yourself to set up an aquarium, you are accepting the responsibility of meeting all of the needs of its inhabitants. The aquarist is responsible for high water quality, proper feeding, correct water temperature, a balanced fish community of the proper density, appropriate habitat and shelter, and sufficient lighting, to name a few. The fish are totally dependent upon you to meet their everyday and emergency needs.

As you gain experience as a fishkeeper, you may go beyond the basic needs and try to breed your fish or establish specialty tanks. But first, it's important to start slowly with your aquarium and develop your talents as an aquarist; you will learn a tremendous amount through your own experiences.

Find a Source of Reliable Advice

Before you buy your aquarium supplies and fish, try to visit all the local aquarium stores and then choose one or two to work with. It is very important to establish a good working relationship with your aquatic dealer, because you need someone to advise you during the setup and maintenance of your system.

You want somebody who maintains a good, clean business, has healthy fish, and is always willing to take time to answer your questions. The good dealer will give you invaluable information on new and reliable products. Choose someone with the right attitude, who will be consistently available to help.

Try to avoid dealers who will not take the time to explain things to you or net the specific fish you desire. Larger dealers with many employees may not meet your needs as a beginner. I've always preferred the smaller pet shops that cater to the needs of aquarists at all levels, are willing to special order supplies, and would rather send you elsewhere than sell you an improper choice. When you settle on one or two dealers, you are ready to begin planning your aquarium.

Chapter 2

Setting Up the Tank

Before you even buy your aquarium, you must decide where you are going to put it. To avoid too much algae growth, do not place the aquarium in direct sunlight. Make sure the aquarium stand will hold the weight of the full aquarium. Water weighs about 8.4 pounds per gallon, so a 30-gallon tank will weigh at least 250 pounds when it's full.

Choose a location that has an adequate electrical supply and is not too far from a source of water. Well-used living areas provide excellent settings for aquariums, because the fish acclimate to people entering and leaving the room. Placing the aquarium in a rarely used area will leave you with fish that are skittish and timid when people approach.

Finally, choose a location that can tolerate a water spill. Even the most meticulous of aquarists spill water around an aquarium, and in many cases water is splashed from a tank. Be firm in your decision about where the tank will be, because once the aquarium is set up it cannot be easily moved.

The Right Tank

The general rule is to buy the largest aquarium you can afford and can accommodate in your home. The reason for this is fairly straightforward: Fish require adequate space to swim and sufficient oxygen to live; both are dictated by the size of the tank. The oxygen content of water is related to the surface area of the tank and the temperature of the water. Warmer water has less oxygen than colder water. Since most freshwater tropical fish prefer water warmer than 75 degrees Fahrenheit, the amount of oxygen in the tank may be limited. The more surface area a tank has, the more room for gas exchange at the surface—more opportunity for oxygen to enter the water and toxic gases to leave. Therefore, the larger the surface area of the tank, the more fish the tank can hold.

Several different methods have been used to determine fish capacity, and there are several general rules. In my opinion, it is better to err on the side of too few fish than too many fish. Most aquarium enthusiasts use fish length and tank volume to estimate the number of fish an aquarium can hold; larger fish consume more oxygen and, therefore, require more aquarium space. The general rule is 1 inch of fish per 4 gallons of water for the first six months. You can gradually increase fish density to 1 inch per 2 gallons after this initial period. For example, a 40-gallon aquarium should contain no more than 10 inches of fish for the first six months. These may comprise ten 1-inch Neon Tetras or five 2-inch Oscars. After six months, additional fish may be added gradually to increase the total number of inches to 20.

Keep in mind, however, that fish grow, and your 2-inch Oscar may be 3 inches after those six months. Also, realize that this general rule does not compensate for the shape of the fish. The width of a fish is called its girth. The girth of an Eel is much smaller than that of an Oscar, and the 3-inch Eel is likely to require less space than the 3-inch Oscar, so the general capacity rule does not apply. If you plan to keep heavier fish (fish with a greater girth), be more conservative in your tank capacity calculations.

Surface area is just as important as overall tank capacity, because the oxygen content of the water is related to the surface area of the tank. The surface area of the tank shown here is much larger than that of the bowl, although they both hold the same amount of water.

Because surface area is so important to the capacity and health of your aquarium, long tanks are much better than tall tanks. Even though both tanks may hold the same volume of water, the upright (tall) tank has much lower carrying capacity of fish because of its smaller surface area.

Once you have decided on the appropriate size of your aquarium, choosing the tank itself is very straightforward. Home aquariums are made of rectangular glass plates sealed with a silicone rubber cement, or of molded acrylic; both have their ups and downs. Glass aquariums are the most common and practical aquariums to buy, and I recommend them for the beginner. They are built for the sole purpose of housing living animals and are, therefore, nontoxic. Glass does not scratch as easily or yellow as acrylic does.

Aquariums with plastic or metal frames are sometimes available, but I have found that this design is not as aesthetically pleasing and that the frames are unnecessary. When choosing your tank, be sure there are no scratches on the glass and that there are no gaps in the silicone that can cause leaks.

C A U T I O N

No Fishbowls, Please

The confined fishbowl is not a proper environment for a fish, whether it's a Goldfish or any other freshwater fish. Water in a fishbowl is unfiltered, not properly aerated, and very poorly maintained. A fishbowl is no more an aquarium than a closet is a house.

The Aquarium Stand

The best support for the heavy weight of the aquarium and all its components is a commercially manufactured aquarium stand. This type of support is built to hold a full aquarium. Homemade stands and other furniture may look sturdy, but can fail under the heavy load. Stand failure can be costly to the aquarist and the homeowner (and the fish), so don't try to save money on your aquarium stand.

If you don't buy a commercially built stand, I recommend that you place under the tank a ⅝-inch sheet of plywood and a ½-inch sheet of polystyrene cut to the dimensions of the tank. These layers will even out any imperfections in the supporting surface and distribute the load of the tank.

The Hood

An essential item for any aquarium is a hood or cover. This important piece of equipment performs a variety of functions. First, it prevents unwanted items from entering the tank and injuring the fish. Second, it prevents overzealous fish from jumping out of the tank. Remember, a fish cannot breathe air, and nothing is worse than finding your pet on the floor next to the aquarium in the morning. The cover also prevents water from splashing the walls and floor, causing damage, and it slows the rate of water evaporation from the tank. Water condenses on the cover and re-enters the tank instead of evaporating; this reduces the necessity of adding more water. Fifth, the hood helps the aquarium retain heat. And finally, the hood keeps water from damaging the aquarium light and prevents a potentially dangerous electrical problem.

A cover will keep all your fish safely in their tank.

The hood is generally fitted to the dimensions of the tank and is adjustable to allow for aquarium accessories. It should be composed of thick (⅛-inch) glass or plastic so it can support the weight of other aquarium components if necessary. It should be segmented so the entire assembly need not be removed to feed the fish or work in the tank.

For the beginner, I strongly recommend the type of hood that also contains the aquarium light. These units are self-contained and are designed to keep water from the lighting unit, minimize danger, and cover the entire tank. If possible, the tank, stand, and hood should be purchased as a package from a single manufacturer. This prevents the problem of mismatched aquarium components, and may also be less expensive.

Creating Proper Water Conditions

Freshwater fish have adapted to a wide variety of habitats around the world. The water in each of these places has its own chemical characteristics to which the species of fishes living there have adapted. These characteristics of water include pH (acidity level), hardness (mineral content), temperature, and oxygen content. In many cases, fish that have adapted to a specific temperature or pH cannot readily live under different conditions.

pH

When we talk about pH, we are really referring to levels of hydrogen ions in solution. Ions are simply atoms with an electrical charge. These hydrogen ions have a positive charge. We measure the number of hydrogen ions on a pH scale.

The pH scale tells us how many hydrogen ions are in your aquarium water and, therefore, how acidic it is. It ranges from 0 to 14. While you would anticipate that a higher number on the scale would mean more hydrogen ions and a more acidic solution, this is not the case. In reality, a lower number on the scale means more hydrogen ions. A pH of 1 is very acidic, pH of 7 is neutral, and a pH of 14 is very alkaline, which is the opposite of acidic. This scale is logarithmic, which means that each number is ten times stronger than the preceding number. For example, a pH of 2 is ten times more acidic than a pH of 3 and one hundred times more acidic than a pH of 4.

The pH of your aquarium water is influenced by a variety of factors, including the amount of carbon dioxide and fish waste in the water. In general, the beginner's aquarium pH should be between 6.5 and 7.5. Commercial test kits that are very simple to use are available at most aquarium supply stores. The pH level in your tank should be monitored every week or two to detect any changes. An abrupt drop in pH may be indicative of an increase in carbon dioxide or fish wastes. An increase in aeration or a partial water change may alleviate the problem.

There are ways to chemically alter the pH in an aquarium. However, unless you are attempting to attain specific pH levels that are dictated by the special needs of certain species of fishes, I do not recommend that you use them.

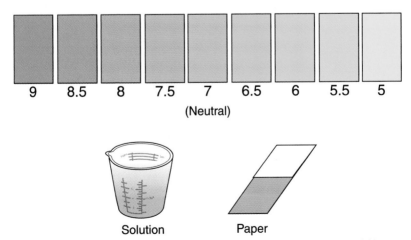

| 9 | 8.5 | 8 | 7.5 | 7 | 6.5 | 6 | 5.5 | 5 |

(Neutral)

Solution   Paper

Determining the pH of the water in your aquarium can be done with simple testing kits available at aquarium supply stores. Results may look something like this.

Hardness

The amount of dissolved mineral salts—that is, calcium and magnesium—in the water is referred to as its hardness. Water with high concentrations of salts is called "hard," while low levels create "soft" water. The degree of hardness scale (dH) ranges from 0 to more than 30 degrees, with 4 to 8 degrees being soft water and 18 to 30 degrees being hard water.

Most freshwater fish do best in water between 3 and 14 degrees of hardness. The beginner generally does not need to alter water hardness unless the local tap water is excessively hard or soft. Commercial kits are now available to test and alter the degree of water hardness. These, too, can be purchased at an aquarium supply store.

The Heater

Based on their temperature preference, fish can be grouped into two general categories: temperate and tropical. Temperate fish include many species that inhabit cooler waters. However, the fish most commonly seen in freshwater aquariums belong to tropical species. The term "tropical" refers to natural habitats where the waters are warm throughout the year. It should come as no surprise, then, that it is necessary to maintain your aquarium within a specific temperature range. This is the job of the aquarium heater.

Most species like their water at a balmy 75 to 79 degrees Fahrenheit. These are Orange Chromides.

This essential piece of equipment maintains your tank at a constant temperature, regardless of the room temperature. With the exception of a few fish, such as the common Goldfish, the species you are likely to keep as a beginner will require the aquarium temperature to be maintained at 75 to 79 degrees Fahrenheit (24 to 26 degrees Celsius). However, this is entirely dependent on the species, and you should consult your

> ## CAUTION
> ### Handle with Care!
> As with all electrical components, please handle your heater with extreme care. Do not switch your submersible heater on until it is submerged in water. Keep *all* your electrical components unplugged until the tank is completely set up and full.

local aquarium dealer or one of the many fish encyclopedias (see the appendix) for specific temperature requirements. Obviously, you should not mix species that have very different temperature requirements.

There are a few types of aquarium heaters available to the aquarist, but the most common is the submersible glass tubular heater with a built-in thermostat. This heater attaches to the side of the tank and has external controls. Once it is properly set, it automatically responds to changes in water temperature and turns itself on and off. If you choose one of these, I recommend that you double-check the accuracy of the dial with a thermometer (see the next section).

In general, you should place your heater close to an area of high circulation so that heated water can be rapidly and evenly distributed throughout the tank. This is usually near the filter system or the airstones.

Heater size largely depends on the size of the aquarium. The general rule is 5 watts of power for every gallon of water. Thus, a 20-gallon tank requires a 100-watt heater. Many fishkeepers recommend that two heaters be used in aquariums over 50 gallons; this allows for more even distribution of heat in the aquarium and also maintains correct temperature if one heater fails. The total required wattage should be divided between the two heaters (so a 50-gallon tank would require two 125-watt heaters, for a total of 250 watts).

Thermometer

To maintain the temperature at suitable levels, all aquarists need an accurate thermometer. There are basically two types of thermometers for the aquarium: the internal floating or fixed thermometer and the external stick-on thermometer. The internal ones tend to be more accurate, and the external ones tend to read a couple of degrees too low.

I recommend two thermometers to enable you to carefully monitor your aquarium temperature as well as to compare the accuracy of each unit. Don't cut corners when it comes to maintaining water temperature. This piece of equipment is very important, yet it does not cost a lot.

Aeration

Fish need to have a lot of oxygen available for respiration. So, although most filters provide water circulation and aeration, it is a very good idea to have an external air pump moving air through one or more airstones in the tank. This is especially true for tanks that are at their fullest carrying capacity. The air pump increases circulation in the tank, promotes oxygen exchange at the surface, and increases the escape of carbon dioxide, carbon monoxide, and free ammonia from the tank. This increase in circulation also acts to mix all the aquarium levels so that a uniform temperature is maintained throughout the tank.

Air Pumps

There are two general air pump designs: the diaphragm type and the piston type. The former is much more common and generally provides enough maintenance–free use for the beginner's aquarium. The piston pump, however, is more powerful and should be used in larger aquariums, particularly if an undergravel filter and multiple airstones need to be powered. The size and power output of air pumps vary. Consult your local dealer to match your aquarium with the proper air pump.

Airstones

An airstone is generally made of porous rock that allows air to pass through it, splitting the airstream into tiny bubbles. Too fine a mist will cause bubbles to adhere to various tank decorations and to fish. You want the bubbles to slowly travel to the surface and agitate the water. Commercially manufactured tank decorations that act as airstones can be purchased at almost any aquarium supply store.

Fish need a lot more air than you might think. This is a Jack Dempsey.

In the wild, fish wastes are flushed away naturally, but in your home tank you must provide filtration.

Air Hose

Your air pump and airstones require an air hose to link the two. This is plastic tubing that delivers air from your pump to the airstone. This should fit snugly at all joints so air does not escape from the system. Air leaks reduce the efficiency of the system (filter and airstone) and may ultimately burn out the pump. Make sure the tubing is manufactured for use in an aquarium; other grades may be toxic to fish.

If you intend to run multiple airstones or additional devices, such as filters, from a single pump, you need one or more air valves. These enable airflow to be directed to multiple devices from a single pump. Using several air valves enables you to turn devices on and off as you like.

Filter Systems

The most important requirement of healthy fish is clean water. Fish in a natural environment are generally exposed to an open system of freshwater in which the products of respiration and digestion are swept away and naturally filtered. In contrast, fish housed in the aquarium live in a closed system where the products of respiration and digestion remain until they are removed. The fishkeeper must take responsibility for removing these wastes and maintaining clean water.

The Nitrogen Cycle

Fish are living creatures that obtain energy from food and burn that energy with the help of oxygen they breathe from the water. These processes generate waste products that are returned to the environment via the gills and the digestive system. These wastes are primarily carbon dioxide and nitrogenous compounds such as ammonia.

In the aquarium, these wastes must be removed. Carbon dioxide generally leaves the water through aeration at the surface or through photosynthesis by aquarium plants. Toxic nitrogenous compounds are converted to less toxic compounds via the nitrogen cycle.

In nature, the nitrogen cycle involves the conversion of toxic nitrogenous wastes and ammonia into harmless products by bacterial colonies. In short, species of bacteria convert solid wastes excreted by fish into ammonia, ammonia into nitrite, and nitrite into nitrate. Nitrate is then used by plants as fertilizer and removed from the water. A healthy aquarium depends greatly on the nitrogen cycle to reduce toxic ammonia into less toxic nitrogen compounds.

The piece of equipment that removes toxic substances from the aquarium is the filter. There are three basic types of filtration: mechanical, chemical, and biological. Mechanical filters physically remove suspended particles from the water by passing it through a fine filter medium. External power filters and canister filters provide rapid mechanical filtration. Chemical filters chemically treat water to remove toxic substances. When you add activated carbon to an external power filter, you are providing chemical filtration. Biological filters use the

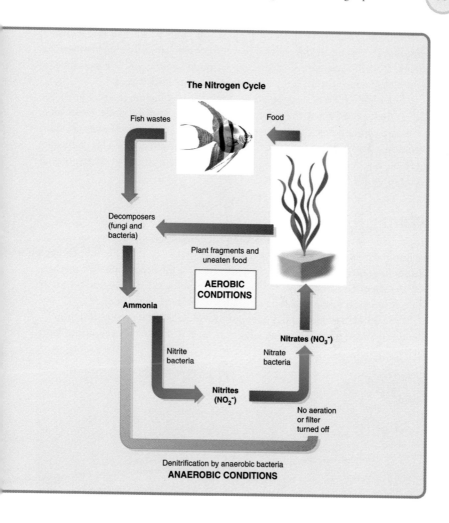

The Nitrogen Cycle

Fish wastes

Food

Decomposers (fungi and bacteria)

Plant fragments and uneaten food

AEROBIC CONDITIONS

Ammonia

Nitrite bacteria

Nitrate bacteria

Nitrates (NO$_3^-$)

Nitrite bacteria

Nitrites (NO$_2^-$)

No aeration or filter turned off

Denitrification by anaerobic bacteria
ANAEROBIC CONDITIONS

nitrogen cycle (see the box above) to remove toxic compounds from the water. An excellent example of a biological filter is the undergravel filter, which draws water through the aquarium substrate. This substrate contains the necessary bacteria to convert nitrogenous wastes to nitrate. Although this type of filtration requires a bit more time to establish a working bacteria colony, it provides the best kind of filtration.

Most commercially manufactured aquarium filters provide all three kinds of filtration. For example, the external power filter mechanically removes particles, chemically removes toxins if it contains activated carbon, and biologically converts nitrogenous wastes via the nitrogen cycle in its filter media.

Some types of filters available to the beginner include the internal box filter, the external power filter, the external canister filter, and the undergravel filter. These are certainly not the only types of filters available, but they are the most common. Choosing the right one for your new aquarium can be a bit confusing, given all the different kinds and manufacturers. Here is a brief description of each type, with the pros and cons.

Internal Box Filter

As the name implies, the internal box filter sits inside the aquarium. An external air pump drives air through the box, drawing water from the aquarium through fibrous filter media and activated charcoal. Layers of filter media provide mechanical and chemical filtration, as well as adequate substrate for biological filtration. Since it is driven by air, this filter circulates and aerates the water.

In my opinion, the box filter does not provide adequate levels of filtration for the average aquarium. Aquarists who start with a tank of 20 gallons or more

Your fish will not thrive without adequate filtration. This is a Thomas' Cichlid.

should not use this type of filter system. It is simply too small to handle the waste and debris that accumulate in the tank, and it has to be cleaned frequently.

External Power Filter

The external power filter is the easiest and least complicated filter system for the beginner's aquarium. These filters provide all three kinds of filtration and are specifically designed to turn over large amounts of water. The external power filter hangs on the side of the tank and is powered by its own motor. Water is drawn into the filter by a U-shaped siphon tube. it passes over layers of fibrous filter material and activated carbon and is returned to the tank via a gravity trickle system or a return pipe. Like the box filter, the power filter circulates the water, providing aeration.

While it works on the same premise as the box filter, the power filter is much more efficient at removing waste and debris from the tank. It does not need to be cleaned as frequently as the box filter. Many models have special filter cartridges that make cleaning these filters extremely easy. In addition, various types of cartridges can be purchased to chemically alter water quality and correct water chemistry problems.

External Canister Filter

The external canister filter is the next step up in power filters. This filter is much larger than the others and is designed to filter large tanks of 50 gallons or more. The canister filter is composed of a large jarlike canister, which generally sits next to the tank. It contains filter media and activated carbon, like the other filters, but has a much more powerful motor for filtering large amounts of water. Water is drawn up by an intake suction line and sent back to the aquarium through a return line. If the return line is properly positioned, water circulation can be provided by these filters. I only recommend this kind of filter for the aquarist with a larger tank.

Undergravel Filter

The undergravel filter is considered by many to be the most effective type of filter because it provides a high level of biological filtration. This filter consists of a plastic plate that sits under the gravel of the tank. Water is drawn through the gravel by pumping air to the bottom of the filter with an external air pump. Some undergravel filters are driven by powerheads mounted on the intake tubes. Both kinds provide excellent water circulation and aeration.

In essence, this filter uses the aquarium gravel itself as the filter media. Thus, very little mechanical filtration is involved and chemical filtration is completely lacking. The undergravel filter relies chiefly on the establishment of a healthy bacterial colony in the gravel. For this reason, certain kinds of gravel are required for this filter, and a longer setup time of many weeks is necessary to establish bacterial colonies. However, once a healthy filtration system is established, this filter can be used for months without intense maintenance and cleaning.

Although this system provides the most valuable kind of filtration, it may be the most complicated for the beginner. Excessive debris in the aquarium can clog the filter bed and must be routinely removed. Aquarists who want to maintain live plants will find that this filter will destroy root systems. In addition, fish may disturb the substrate and upset the filtration bed. The novice would be better off with an external power filter.

Aquarium Lighting

Proper lighting is a necessary component for every aquarium, because it provides illumination and promotes plant growth. While lighting from the sun provides a natural setting, it will also promote excessive algae growth and alter the temperature of your tank, so aquariums should be placed away from sunlit areas. Instead, you'll need a commercially manufactured aquarium light.

Like all aquarium components, the aquarium light comes in a variety of types and forms. By far the most common is the fluorescent light that fits snugly on top of the aquarium hood and provides even, cool illumination. There are several types of fluorescent bulbs that can create special effects in your aquarium. If you intend to maintain plants, use fluorescent tubes that cover the ideal spectral range of plants and promote plant growth. For example, red and blue light enhances the colors of red and blue fish, while promoting plant growth.

Your aquarium supply dealer carries a full variety of fluorescent light bulbs. If you buy your fish tank with a hood and light canopy (as I recommended), this is most likely to be a fluorescent light. If you do not buy a tank, cover, and light package, make sure the light you buy extends across the entire length of the tank. This is by far the most efficient and economical form of lighting available for your tank, and I thoroughly recommend it.

When choosing your lighting, consider the depth of your aquarium and the number of live plants you intend to grow. These two aspects of your tank dictate the power, number, and type of bulbs you buy. The general rule is 2 to 2.5 watts per gallon of water. However, if you intend to maintain large numbers of live

The Peacock Gudgeon is a very colorful freshwater fish.

plants, you should consult some of the sources listed in the appendix before buying your lighting system.

An oft-overlooked component to the lighting system is an on-off timer switch. Tropical freshwater fish come from regions where daylight ranges from ten to fifteen hours a day. A timer switch automatically turns on and shuts off your lighting system so that a consistent day length can be maintained. A twelve-hour day length is generally recommended for most aquariums.

You should always try not to startle your fish, so avoid suddenly switching the light on or off. To better simulate a normal sunset, switch off the aquarium light about an hour before other room lights are turned off. This little detail will help keep your fish happy and well adjusted.

Inside the Tank

Since your community aquarium will feature a variety of fish from several habitats, it is best to create an aquascape that is pleasing to the human eye as well as pleasing to the fish. This requires a variety of components that meet the habitat needs of its inhabitants.

Decorations

Aquarium supply stores sell a variety of tank decorations that enhance the habitat for your fish. Some are plastic or ceramic creations and others are simply attractive rocks and stones. By buying these tank decorations from the dealer, you are avoiding contaminating your tank with toxic substances and water chemistry-modifying agents. Avoid the temptation to collect your own rocks until you know how to identify each kind and its influence on your aquarium.

Before buying any decorations for your aquarium, take the time to design the kind of setting you want to build for your fish. In their natural habitats, fish have access to shelter as well as sufficient swimming space. Caves and rock ledges mimic your fish's natural habitat and increase their sense of security and well-being.

Gravel

The bottom substrate of your aquarium is gravel. The gravel is a natural addition that provides anchorage to plants and other decorations and also provides a home for useful bacteria that power the nitrogen cycle and rid the aquarium of toxic wastes. Be careful when choosing a substrate for the new aquarium. Certain kinds of materials can alter the chemistry of the aquarium, creating water hardness problems.

I thoroughly discourage collecting gravel or aquarium decorations from the wild. Rather, purchase them from an aquarium supply dealer. As you develop a better understanding of the water hardness in your area and its effects on your aquarium, you may be able to add more natural components.

All aquarium stores sell gravel for the freshwater aquarium. Be sure not to buy coral sand, which is recommended for saltwater aquarium use only. Gravel comes in a variety of sizes, ranging from coarse to very fine. If you intend to use an undergravel filter, fine gravel will clog it and compromise its effectiveness. It will also harm the mouths and digestive systems of bottom feeding fish. On the other hand, if grains are too large, fish that tend to dig will not be able to move the substrate. This is particularly important for breeding fish. Medium pea-size

Buy your aquarium gravel from a dealer. Items collected from the wild can leech minerals into your tank. This is a fancy Goldfish.

gravel is a good choice. Gravel also comes in a variety of colors, ranging from bright reds to natural tones of gray. This decision is based solely on your taste, but be mindful of the color of your lighting when choosing your gravel colors.

The gravel should be about 1.5 to 2 inches deep on the aquarium bottom. If you use an undergravel filter, 2.5 to 3 inches is recommended. It is always best to buy a bit extra so that when you aquascape your tank, you have enough to sculpt the bottom.

Plants

The first decision you must make about plants is whether to add artificial or live plants to your aquarium. My personal feeling is that there are enough problems you will encounter in the first year of maintaining an aquarium, and live plants need not be added to the list of things that can go wrong. While live plants are more natural looking and provide an excellent service of reducing carbon dioxide and using up nitrates in the tank, they also have very specific needs that must be met. If proper care is not taken, they will die and contribute to water quality problems that you are desperately trying to avoid.

If you choose artificial plants, there are a great many varieties at the aquarium supply store that you can select from. The more expensive forms look real and

Artificial plants provide a lovely backdrop for this Angelfish.

enable you to have plant life in your aquarium (which the fish like, because they need hiding and resting places) without the risk of degrading water quality.

If you want to graduate to live plants or start out with them, it is important to understand how underwater plants grow and what kinds are available to the freshwater aquarist. Plants remove carbon dioxide and add oxygen to the water during photosynthesis and use nitrates generated by the nitrogen cycle. They need light for photosynthesis. In low light or in darkness, plants do not photosynthesize; instead, they produce carbon dioxide like fish. This will influence the aquarium pH and overall water quality. That is why it is very important to provide adequate illumination and sufficient filtration if live plants are added to your tank.

Plants add an additional source of food for fish that browse on vegetable matter or feed on algae colonies that develop on the plants' leaves. In addition, plants are a good indicator of the health of your aquarium, since they are the first to die if anything goes awry.

According to Barry James, author of *A Fishkeeper's Guide to Aquarium Plants,* aquatic plants can be divided into several types based on their form, size, and growing characteristics.

Floating plants   Floating plants float on or just below the surface; their root system dangles in the water. These plants provide shade to other plants and fish in the aquarium. A common species of floating plant is *Riccia fluitans,* which is fast growing and provides an ideal spawning habitat.

Bunch plants   Bunch plants reproduce off a single stem and quickly envelop a tank. The long stems and leaves, arranged in pairs or whorls, make these plants ideal for planting as a background in the aquarium. *Egeria densa* is a bunch plant that is great for beginners. It grows fast, cleans the water, and produces a lot of oxygen. *Vallisneria spiralis* is another bunch plant that is very hardy, grows to about 15 inches, and spreads rapidly in dense clumps.

Specimen plants   Specimen plants are large plants that should be planted in the middleground to create a striking design. Popular species of specimen plants include the Amazon sword plant, *Echinodorus* species. These are extremely tolerant plants with leaves that are broad in the middle and tapered at each end.

Deep marginal plants   Deep marginal plants grow from bulbs or tubers and produce long stems. They are ideal plants for the middleground, background, or back corners of the tank. Species of *Nymphaea* and *Aponogeton* are ideal deep marginal plants that have modest care requirements. *Nymphaea,* however, are water lilies that, when allowed to grow unchecked, tend to block out light from other plants.

Middleground plants   Middleground plants in the form of rosettes are similar to but smaller than specimen plants. These include *Cryptocoryne affinis,* which grows to 12 inches tall and is very suitable for grouping. *Cryptocoryne* species are slow growers and take time to establish themselves. They are also easily affected by disease and sometimes require iron supplements.

Foreground plants   Foreground plants are small plants that are ideally suited to the foreground of the tank. These include *Eleocharis* species, with their bunched, grasslike appearance.

Certainly, this is just a smattering of the species of plants that are available in most aquarium supply stores. If you are interested in maintaining live plants in a new aquarium, I thoroughly recommend that you consult the references listed in the appendix before selecting a plant species.

Just as different species of fishes have specific temperature and water quality requirements, so do the various species of plants. The species outlined above are well suited to the

A variety of plants gives your aquarium a natural look.

Take care of your plants as well as you do your fish. This is a Redline Pike Cichlid.

aquarium of the novice aquarist. However, aquariums with live plants generally require more light than those with artificial plants. This must be considered when setting up the aquarium. In addition, plants generally thrive in finer substrate than that recommended for the average community tank. This, too, should be taken into account when selecting the types of fish that will inhabit your tank.

Select your plants carefully. Make sure the root system looks healthy and the leaves are free of brown decay. Get to know a little about each plant species, its maximum size, and light and water requirements. You don't want to add a plant that will outgrow or overly shade your aquarium.

Be sure to take proper care of your plants once they are added to your aquarium. Some species require routine fertilization. This can be accomplished by using commercially available liquid, tablet, and substrate fertilizers. Be sure to read the instructions carefully, as the frequency and amount of fertilization depends on which product you buy. In addition to fertilizer, routine cleaning of plants is essential. About once a week remove dead leaves by hand from plants. This prevents debris from degrading water quality and inhibiting photosynthesis. Depending on how fast your plants grow, you need to frequently trim and prune them to prevent them from overgrowing in your aquarium. Remember, plants use oxygen at night and, therefore, compete with your fish for oxygen.

Other Accessories

As you develop your talents as an aquarist, a number of accessories for your tank can make your job easier and help you maintain a happy, healthy aquarium. The following are a couple of items that give you a head start.

I have already mentioned the importance of **water quality test kits.** Make sure when you buy your complete aquarium setup that these are not left out. Test kits that measure pH, hardness, and nitrogen compounds are a must. The nitrogen kits should include tests for ammonia, nitrite, and nitrate.

There are a couple of handy accessories that help keep your tank clean. An **algae sponge** or aquarium cleaner is a sponge attached to a long handle that is used for scraping down the inside of the tank without having to empty the aquarium. The sponge easily scrapes off algae but does not scratch the tank. A **magnetic aquarium cleaner** is also an effective cleaning tool. This uses two magnets with attached cleaning surfaces. One magnet is kept outside the tank and the other is controlled on the inside walls of the tank by the outside magnet.

An **aquarium vacuum** is a must for the beginner. This is usually a hand pump siphon that enables you to extract larger debris from the aquarium floor without having to submerge your hands or use a net.

You will definitely need a **fishnet**

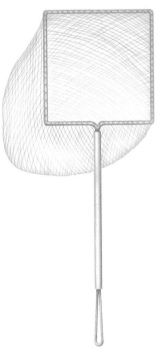

Make sure the size of your fishnet suits the size of your fish and your tank.

or two. It's better to have a couple of sizes handy, depending on the size of your tank and the size of your fish. Too small a net does not allow you to corner a fish, and too large a net is difficult to maneuver in the tank. You will use a fishnet more often than you think. It comes in very handy when you need to remove a fish that is ill or dead or an aggressive fish, or when the time has come to clean the tank and remove all the fish.

There are other items for routine aquarium maintenance that you want to have within arm's reach. Set aside a **5-gallon bucket** and a **siphon hose** for use only with your aquarium. Then you will not have to prepare a clean bucket and hose every time you need one, and it will reduce the likelihood of introducing toxic agents into the aquarium (which is much more likely if you use a different bucket or hose each time).

A colored backdrop conceals the fixtures around your aquarium, while natural decorations will give fish like this Shelldwelling Cichlid places to rest and hide.

Although not an essential piece of equipment, an **aquarium backdrop** or screen is preferred by many aquarists. The aquarium backdrop is a paper or plastic backing that you place on the exterior back wall of the aquarium. This conceals tubes, filters, pumps, and other fixtures that are usually kept behind the tank. Since many tanks are placed against the wall, the backdrop prevents you from seeing the paint or wallpaper on the wall behind the tank as well. Aquarium backdrops come in a variety of colors, shades, and scenes. Choose one that you find most appealing and that fits the decor of your aquarium.

Before you buy the decorative components of your tank, take the time to sketch out on paper just how you want your aquarium to look. Include the gravel, plants, decorations, and the backdrop. Keep in mind that fish require shelters as well as swimming space. Therefore, visualize your aquarium with rocks, caves, and areas of refuge. Once you have a conceptual design in mind and on paper, setting up your aquarium will be much easier.

Chapter 3

Setting Up Your Aquarium

The first step in properly setting up your new aquarium is to assemble all the components in the area where you want the aquarium to be. (Remember to follow the guidelines I outlined in chapter 2 when you're choosing the right place for your aquarium.) Inventory the various components of the aquarium system and make sure you're not missing anything.

Successful Setup

Once you are confident that everything is in order, take the following steps to set up your aquarium.

1. Make sure everything is clean. Give the gravel, tank, filter, heater, aquarium decorations, artificial plants, and anything else you expect to put in the tank a thorough rinsing with clean, warm water. Residues, dirt, and toxic agents can accumulate on your equipment between the time it is manufactured and the time it gets to your home. When it comes to cleaning aquarium decorations such as rocks and wood, use a scrubbing brush to remove dirt. Never use any kind of soap when cleaning your aquarium components; soap can cause immediate water quality problems.
2. Place the tank on its stand exactly where you want it to be. Don't expect to move the tank once it is filled with water! Now it's time to begin assembling the interior of your aquarium. Aquascape your tank beginning with the bottom layer, the gravel. If you are going to use an undergravel filter,

remember to add it before gently pouring in the gravel. Terrace the gravel so that it is higher in the back of the tank than in the front.

3. Add any larger pieces of rock, wood, etc. Remember to follow your plan, making changes where you see fit. Don't attempt to add plants (either real or artificial) or smaller decorations until the water is added to the tank, because they may be disrupted by the filling process. Remember to leave spaces for heaters, filters, and other equipment.

4. Add the airstones to the aquarium, taking the opportunity to conceal the air supply tubing behind larger decorations.

5. Add water to the tank. To avoid disrupting your aquascape, place a clean plate or bowl on the substrate and pour the water onto it. In most households, tap water will be fine. If you suspect your tap water is excessively hard or soft, or contains high levels of chloramine, check with your local water company. In these cases, you may need to buy water or chemically treat your tap water. In most cases, the aquarium aging process, combined with filtration, will alleviate minor tap water problems.

6. Place the filter and heater in the tank and position them. Prepare the filter by following the manufacturer's instructions regarding filter media before setting it on or in the tank. Position the heater in a way that maximizes its output—near sources of water circulation such as filter outlets or airstones.

7. Place the smaller decorations in the tank, add the thermometer, and fine-tune your aquascape. Add artificial plants according to your plan. If you

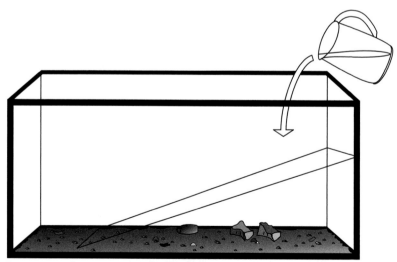

Pour water into the aquarium over a slanted surface so you don't disrupt your aquascape.

are going to add live plants, it's best to wait until your tank is up and running, so the conditions will be right. Once added to the tank, live plants may need to be weighted down until root systems are well established.

8. Fit the hood, making sure the external components and electrical equipment are properly placed. Add the light on top of the canopy and make sure it is connected correctly.

9. When you are confident that the electrical wiring is safely insulated from sources of water, plug the aquarium units in and turn on the system. Make sure the heater is properly adjusted; this may take a day or so. Check the operation of the filter, air pumps, and light.

10. Let the tank water mature before adding any fish.

Aquarium Maturation

When you have completed all these steps, you may have a tank filled with water but you do not yet have the working, well-balanced, artificial habitat that we call an aquarium. At this point, you need to let the tank mature. Remember, fish require suitable water quality with appropriate levels of water pH and hardness. Your tap water may contain treatment additives that can harm your fish. In addition, your new tank does not have a well-established nitrogen cycle.

Water circulation, temperature regulation, and filtration will help your water mature; how long it takes will depend on the type of setup you have. A new undergravel filter takes between four and six weeks to fully establish itself. Many experts believe you should wait a minimum of ten to fourteen days before introducing fish into your aquarium. On the other hand, I have added fish to a new tank in as little as one to two days. It depends on when your pH and hardness stabilize and how well you have established the nitrogen cycle. There are commercial treatments available that will accelerate the maturation process. If you decide to use one of these, get advice from your local dealer and read the instructions carefully.

> **TIP**
>
> **Bringing Your Fish Home**
>
> When you bring a fish home, the aquarium supply dealer will put it in a plastic bag with water and enough oxygen for a short trip. Ask to have the plastic bag placed inside a dark opaque bag. Keeping the fish in the dark will help reduce the stress of the trip. You must resist the temptation to take the fish out and gawk at it. Bringing the fish from the dark into the light and into the dark again can put the fish in shock. Keep it in the bag until you get home.

Even these Goldfish require specific levels of water pH and hardness, so let your aquarium mature before adding your fish.

It is important to test your water daily to determine when you can add fish. In general, once pH and hardness have stabilized, in two to four days, the next step is to fuel the nitrogen cycle. This can be done by introducing a few very hardy fish, such as common Goldfish, into the tank. These fish will produce the necessary ammonia to help establish bacterial colonies that comprise the nitrogen cycle.

Once the fish have been introduced, it is important to continue to monitor ammonia, nitrite, and nitrate levels. Within a few days you will see ammonia and nitrite levels begin to climb rapidly, and nitrate will remain low. If you introduce the fish too soon, they may be poisoned by high ammonia levels. This means the bacterial colonies that convert these compounds into the less harmful nitrate are not yet established. In most cases, if you wait a few days before introducing your starter fish, this will not happen.

Gradually, in about one to two weeks, your ammonia levels will stabilize, nitrite will decrease, and nitrate will increase. It is time to add more fish. Add just a couple of fish every few days. Remember to calculate the maximum number of fish your tank can handle (see chapter 2) and use this number conservatively. Continue to monitor ammonia, nitrite, and nitrate levels throughout this period. If a sudden peak occurs in ammonia or nitrite, stop adding fish until that peak diminishes.

Adding Fish to the Tank

When you leave the aquarium supply store, your fish will be packed in plastic bags. Make sure the dealer fills the air space in the bag with oxygen. Take care not to disturb or shock your fish during transport. Follow these steps when you get home.

1. Float the plastic bag containing your fish in the tank so that the temperature in the bag can acclimate to that in the aquarium. Let the bag sit in the tank for at least ten to fifteen minutes.
2. Open the bag to let some fresh air in, then seal it again. To ensure the fish will not be shocked by the aquarium water, make sure that both have a temperature within a degree of each other. Add a handful of water from your aquarium to the bag and let it sit for another ten to fifteen minutes.
3. Now you can add the fish to the tank by opening the bag and gently inverting it into the tank, letting the fish out.

Make sure your aquarium contains all the necessary elements and is chemically stabilized before you begin to add fish.

Part II
Freshwater Aquarium Fish

Chapter 4

Common Freshwater Fish Families

C hances are you will have freshwater tropical fish in your new aquarium. Although most are now bred in captivity for the aquarium trade, in their natural habitats they are found throughout the world. The diversity of these fish is amazing and can be daunting. To make these fish easier to understand and sort out, scientists have classified them into various groups.

A particular species has a common name, which can differ depending on the region or the language. However, every species also has a scientific name that is used to identify that species in all places and in all languages. The scientific name of a species is based on Latin, and is made up of the genus and the species. For example, the scientific name of the Neon Tetra is *Paracheirodon innesi* and the Cardinal Tetra's is *Paracheirodon axelrodi*. The first name is the genus (a grouping of very similar species) to which both species belong (in this case, they are both Tetra). If you look at these fish, you can see that they are extremely similar. The second name refers only to that species and no other. Similar genera (the plural of genus) are classified into families.

In general, most experts prefer to combine freshwater aquarium fish families into two major groups: livebearers and egglayers. This is based purely on the method these fish use to reproduce. In the rest of this chapter, I am going to outline the major families of each group. I have taken the liberty of grouping families that have similar characteristics.

This is by no means a complete list of tropical freshwater fish families—only those you are most likely to encounter. When I say a single species has additional varieties or strains, it refers to the selective breeding of a species for certain characteristics and to establish a new variety (not a new species). For example, the Goldfish, *Carassius auratus,* has been selectively bred to develop more than 125 recognized varieties.

Livebearers

The livebearers give birth to live young. They include four major families—Anablepidae, Goodeidae, Hemirhamphidae, and Poeciliidae—that are kept in captivity. These are the common aquarium fishes known as Guppies, Mollies, Platys, and Swordtails, as well as the various breeds and strains of each. These are especially hardy fish that breed readily in captivity. The males of these families are easily recognizable by their gonopodium. This modified pelvic fin is used by the male to mate with the female.

Egglayers

Most species of fish lay eggs. Different egglayers have different reproduction strategies, some of which involve watching the eggs and even caring for the young. Chapter 9 will explain more about egglayers and how they reproduce.

Guppies, like many other livebearers, are hardy fish that breed readily in captivity.

The Chen's Sucker Loach can grow to 2.5 inches long.

Barbs and Rasboras

These fishes belong to the closely related families Cyprinidae and Cobitidae, which contain more than 2,000 species of fishes. Loaches, such as the Clown Loach from India, are very popular aquarium fish in the Cobitidae family. Cyprinid fishes include the Tiger Barb from Indonesia and the Zebra Danio from India. The Red-tailed Shark, which is not a shark but actually a Rasbora, is also a member of this family; it originates in Thailand.

Mormyrids

Commonly known as the Elephantnose fish, species of the family Mormyridae have extended mouths like an elephant's trunk. Found in Africa, these fish use this modified mandible as a sensory organ. They also possess an organ near their tail that generates weak electrical signals. When an Elephantnose becomes nervous, its electric pulse rate increases. The continuous pulsing of the electric organ can disturb other aquarium fish, as well as other Elephantnose fish.

Catfish

There are fifteen families and 2,000 species of Catfish that are found in the aquarium trade. The so-called armored Catfish (Loricariidae, Callichthyidae) include the popular Plecostomus fish and other algae eaters found in home aquariums. This group also includes the 148 species of Corydoras Catfish, with their large heads and short bodies. These South American Catfish are known for their propensity to feed on the substrate, thereby cleaning the tank bottom. Other common Catfish, such as the Banjo Catfish, the Naked Catfish, the Glass Catfish, and the Pim Catfish, belong to other Catfish families. Most of these are peaceful and easily adapt to a community tank.

Characins

This group contains seventeen fish families of fish more commonly known as the Tetras. There are more than 1,300 species of Tetras, originating mostly in South America but also Africa. Common characteristics of this group include having a toothed jaw and an adipose fin or second dorsal fin. In many species, males can be distinguished from females by the hooklike spines on their anal fin or projecting from the base of their tail. These fish generally form schools in their natural habitat.

Two of the most popular Characins with very different dispositions are the Neon Tetra and the Red-bellied Piranha. A small school of Neon Tetras is an attractive addition to the aquarium, but Piranhas belong in a single-species tank. Overall, most members of this group are peaceful and make excellent additions to a community aquarium.

This Paleatus Corydoras is one of 148 species of Corydoras Catfish.

Cichlids

The family Cichlidae contains more than 1,300 species of fishes originating from Central and South America, parts of the Caribbean, southern India, and across Africa. Cichlids (pronounced *sick-lids*) inhabit a wide range of habitats throughout these areas, including saltwater and hot springs (104 degrees Fahrenheit). Most Cichlids are small to medium in size with a single dorsal fin composed of spines and soft rays. Some species, like the freshwater Angelfish, are compressed laterally and have long, ornate fins.

Common Cichlids include the Jack Dempsey, Oscar, Angelfish, and Discus. Temperament in this group ranges from pugnacious and intolerant to very peaceful. Cichlids can be extremely territorial and some mate for life. Care should be taken when selecting Cichlids for a community aquarium.

Killifish

These fish belong primarily to two families, the Aplocheilidae and the Cyprinodontidae. They are a very diverse group with more than 400 species, spanning all the continents except Australia and Antarctica. Killifish have permeated saltwater, brackish, and freshwater habitats throughout their range. Distinctive rounded scales and a lateral line system only around the head are characteristic features of this group. Some of the more common members of this group include the Lyretails, Rivulus, and Lampeyes.

Discus are members of the large Cichlid family.

Labyrinth Fish

This group is named for the special organ inside their head that is called the labyrinth. This organ enables the fish to breathe in air at the water's surface. Inhaled air is pressed into the labyrinth, where oxygen is drawn out. This enables these fish to survive in oxygen-depleted waters.

Many of these fishes come from Thailand, Indonesia, Cambodia, and Malaysia. There are four families of

This Blue Gourami, like all other labyrinth fish, possesses a special organ that enables it to breathe air at the surface.

labyrinth fish, but only two, Belontiidae and Helostomatiidae, have species that are kept in captivity.

The most popular of the labyrinth fish belong to the family Belontiidae, which includes the Gouramis, Paradise Fish, and Bettas. The Paradise Fish is extremely hardy, but becomes very territorial in an aquarium as an adult. The Betta is better known as the Siamese Fighting Fish, so-named because the males fight and tear each other's fins to shreds. Although sometimes displayed in very small fishbowls, these fish should not be kept in less than a liter of water; they are very sensitive to temperature changes. The Gouramis are very popular additions to a community tank. They are peaceful fish with ornate fins and prefer heavy vegetation.

The only member of the family Helostomatiidae maintained in captivity is the popular Kissing Fish. Native to Thailand, these fish are actually displaying aggression when "kissing" another member of the species.

Rainbowfish

This group comprises three families (Melanotaeniidae, Atherinidae, and Psuedomugilidae), mostly originating from New Guinea and eastern Australia. Members of this group are peaceful, active schooling fish with oval, laterally compressed bodies. A common member of this group is the Splendid Rainbow.

And the Rest

The groups of families I have reviewed are those most commonly seen in aquarium supply stores. There are at least forty families of fish kept in aquariums that I have not covered here. They are so diverse in form and behavior that a discussion of each would require too much space. I highly recommend that you consult one of the fish encyclopedias listed in the appendix. These references not only describe each species available to the aquarist, but also list the specific aquarium requirements of each.

Knifefish

The unique group of Knifefish comprises four families. The Speckled Knifefish (Apteronotidae), the Banded Knifefish (Gymnotidae), and the American Knifefish (Rhamphichthyidae) are found in Central and South America. The fourth family, Notopteridae, comes from the fresh waters of Africa and Asia. These fish are so-named for their laterally compressed, blade-shaped tapered bodies. Most species are nocturnal and peaceful, but they should be kept with fish of similar size. Some of the Notopterid Knifefish, however, are aggressive and are best kept alone.

Chapter 5

Choosing Fish for Your Aquarium

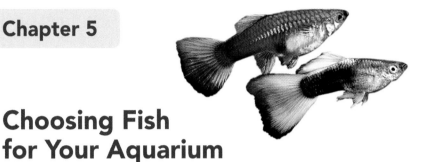

Throughout this book, I have referred to your aquarium as a community tank. The community tank contains different species of compatible fishes, while the species tank contains only a single species of fish. I believe beginners should start with a community; the species tank concept is best for those who want to maintain fish that require special tank conditions or are extremely aggressive.

There are a wide variety of fishes that are well suited for a community aquarium. The important thing to do is balance the types of fishes in your tank. You will recall that fish species have adapted to a variety of lifestyles and habitats. There are fish that live in the topwater, fish that live in the midwater, and fish that prefer the bottom. In a community tank, you want to re-create this kind of environment by having fish spread throughout the tank on every level.

In addition, many fish species school. This can be a very attractive addition to a community tank. These schooling fish should never be kept alone; they need to be in groups of at least five or six individuals.

As I mentioned in the previous chapter, some fish tend to be aggressive. These critters should be avoided, because a single antagonistic fish in a community tank can wreak havoc on the other inhabitants.

Another aspect that the novice tends to overlook is the maximum size of a particular species. A fish will grow continuously throughout its life; some species grow faster than others. You don't want to put a fish in your tank that will grow to 12 inches in less than a year. This will not only disrupt your aquarium capacity, but the larger fish will undoubtedly dominate the tank. Some species are very compatible with other species when they are juveniles but become solitary and aggressive as adults. These fish do not belong in a peaceful community tank.

Picking Out Your Fish

Be selective when you get to the aquarium supply store. Buy fish only from healthy looking aquariums with clear water, clean panes, and no dead fish in the tank. Make sure the fish you want is healthy looking. If the fish has any cuts, scrapes, or fin problems, don't buy it. Watch for possible signs of disease such as white granular spots, cottony white patches, frayed fins, or dull skin. Watch the behavior of the fish. Healthy fish swim in a lively manner and are not shy.

Most fishkeepers agree that it is important to introduce your fish to the aquarium in batches, buying fish in small lots every ten to fourteen days. This allows fish to acclimate to one another and avoids aggressive behavior toward a single fish when it is introduced.

When your tank is fully established and the water chemistry is balanced, you are ready to stock your aquarium. I thoroughly recommend that you have a game plan in mind. Don't blindly go to your aquarium supply dealer and look for fish to fill your tank. This can result in fish incompatibility. Instead, decide beforehand what fish species you want. Take some of my suggestions in this chapter. Consult with some of the fish encyclopedias listed in the appendix. In other words, establish a good list of potential fish that you want to introduce into your aquarium. Remember to choose a variety of species that will live throughout the water column from the top to the bottom.

The Best Aquarium Fish for Beginners

The following is a list of species that are particularly easy to care for. They are well suited for a beginner's community tank where pH ranges from 6.5 to 7.5 and temperature is maintained between 75 and 79 degrees Fahrenheit. I have arranged these fish according to the part of your tank they are most likely to inhabit: topwater, midwater, and bottom.

Topwater Fish

The topwater fish are not restricted to the upper levels of the tank, but are more likely to be seen there. For these species, feeding and spawning, in particular, occur at or near the surface of the water.

Guppy *(Poecilia reticulata)*

Family: Poeciliidae
Distribution: From Central America to Brazil
Size: Males 1.5 inches, Females 2.5 inches
Food: Omnivorous
Temperature: 64 to 81 degrees Fahrenheit

Guppies prefer to live in small groups.

This species is a definite favorite among beginners because it is a very hardy fish that gives birth to live young every month. The male is very colorful, with ornate fins and a gonopodium; females are dull in coloration. Selective breeding has resulted in the production of more than 100 varieties. These fish are vigorous, schooling swimmers and prefer small groups of four to six. Provide plenty of cover and floating plants and you may be able to successfully raise the fry (newborn fish).

Green Swordtail *(Xiphophorus hellerii)*

Family: Poeciliidae
Distribution: Central America
Size: Males 4 inches, Females 4.5 inches
Food: Omnivorous
Temperature: 68 to 79 degrees Fahrenheit

Swordtails help your tank by eating algae.

The Green Swordtail is another popular community fish because it breeds readily in captivity. The males have a long swordlike extension on the lower part of their tail fin that develops as the fish matures (hence the species' common name). The males can be temperamental and will harass the females, so it is best to have the females outnumber the males; males will quarrel with each other as well. These fish breed every twenty-eight days at 74 degrees Fahrenheit. As with the Guppy, dense vegetation provides cover for developing fry. Another benefit of this species is its tendency to consume algae.

Black Molly (Poecilia sphenops)

Family: Poeciliidae
Distribution: From Mexico to Colombia
Size: 2.5 inches
Food: Omnivorous
Temperature: 64 to 82 degrees Fahrenheit

The Black Molly is a hybrid, developed for the aquarium trade.

The Black Molly is actually a hybrid of the original variety, the Mexican Molly. The many varieties prefer temperatures on the upper end of the range. Other varieties include the Green, Marbled, Albino, and Lyretail Mollies. This species is another livebearer that is gentle and is basically a vegetable eater. Like the Swordtail, the Molly will consume aquarium algae, keeping it in check. This species is lively and prefers schooling in small groups of four to six members. Although not as hardy as other livebearers, the Molly prospers if aquarium conditions are kept constant.

Platy (Xiphophorus maculatus)

Family: Poeciliidae
Distribution: From Mexico and Guatemala to Honduras
Size: Males 4 inches, Females 4.5 inches
Food: Omnivorous
Temperature: 72 to 79 degrees Fahrenheit

This Red Wag Platy is an ideal community fish.

The Platy belongs to the same genus as the Swordtail and is therefore a very close relative. Some consider it to be the ideal community fish. As with most livebearers, many color varieties have been commercially bred for the home aquarium. Plenty of cover in dense vegetation will lead to successful breeding and the survival of the fry in a community tank. The Platy consumes algae and prefers to live in small groups of five to seven fish. A very similar species, the Variable Platy *(Xiphophorus variatus)*, is equally hardy and is well suited for a community tank.

Zebra Danio *(Danio rerio)*

Family: Cyprinidae
Distribution: India
Size: 2.5 inches
Food: Omnivorous
Temperature: 64 to 75 degrees Fahrenheit

The Zebra Danio is an active schooling fish.

The torpedo-shaped Danios are very active schooling fish that should be kept in groups of at least seven or eight. This egglayer has been commercially bred to both albino and long-finned strains. Males are generally slimmer than females, and usually remain loyal to one female once they have spawned. A similar species is the Pearl Danio *(Danio albolineatus)*.

White Cloud Mountain Minnow *(Tanichthys albonubes)*

Family: Cyprinidae
Distribution: Southern China
Size: 1.5 inches
Food: Omnivorous
Temperature: 64 to 72 degrees Fahrenheit

This White Cloud Mountain Minnow prefers cooler water.

This very undemanding, active fish should be kept in a group of eight or more. Males are slimmer and have more intense coloration than females. Note that these peaceful fish prefer cooler water and should only be kept in temperatures less than 72 degrees Fahrenheit.

Common Hatchetfish
(Gasteropelecus sternicla)

Family: Gasteropelecidae
Distribution: Brazil, Guyana, and Surinam
Size: 2.5 inches
Food: Carnivorous
Temperature: 73 to 79 degrees Fahrenheit

Common Hatchetfish are excellent jumpers, so be sure to keep your aquarium covered.

This surface dweller and its close relative, the Marbled Hatchetfish *(Carnegiella strigata),* are Characins that need to be kept in schools of at least six. The unusually deep body of these species makes them an interesting addition to any community aquarium. All Hatchets are excellent jumpers, so be sure to keep the hood in place on the tank. A few floating plants will provide adequate cover for these gentle fish.

Siamese Fighting Fish
(Betta splendens)

Family: Osphronemidae
Distribution: Cambodia and Thailand
Size: 3 inches
Food: Carnivorous
Temperature: 75 to 84 degrees Fahrenheit

Male Siamese Fight Fish will fight to the death, so you can keep only one male per tank.

This beautiful labyrinth fish is a popular addition to the community aquarium. Selective breeding over the years has enhanced the brilliant ornate fins of the males. However, only one male may be kept per aquarium, otherwise vicious fighting will occur; duels between males can result in death. Males are generally peaceful with other species, unless they have similar fin veils. The smaller, shorter-finned females are drabber but may be kept together in a community tank. This egglaying species builds a bubblenest at the surface of the aquarium, where the eggs are guarded by the males.

Midwater Fish

Many of the midwater swimmers belong to the groups of fishes known as the Cyprinids and the Characins. Most do best in schools of eight or more individuals. With this in mind, the beginner should consider having only one or two species of schooling midwater fish.

Rosy Barb *(Puntius conchonius)*

Family: Cyprinidae
Distribution: Northern India
Size: 3 inches
Food: Omnivorous
Temperature: 64 to 72 degrees
Fahrenheit

The Rosy Barb is most colorful in cooler waters.

Barbs get their name from the short threadlike barbels that act as sensory organs on either side of their mouths and sometimes on their lips. Their vigor and agility in the midwater of the tank contribute greatly to the vitality of your aquarium. Many Barbs, however, can harm smaller fish and fish with ornate, veil-like fins. The Rosy Barb is a very peaceful species that adapts well to a community aquarium. However, it prefers cooler water than other community fish and is most colorful in those conditions.

A related species, the Tiger Barb *(Puntius tetrazona),* has a bit wilder disposition when introduced singly or as a pair. This fish will wreak havoc among other occupants, nipping fins and harassing them. However, if kept in schools of eight or more, they establish a hierarchy and generally leave the other fish alone. It is recommended that schools contain both the more colorful males and the heavier females. This Indonesian species prefers warmer water in the range of 68 to 79 degrees Fahrenheit.

The Ruby Barb *(Puntius nigrofasciatus)* of Sri Lanka also prefers warmer water and, when in the company of other Barbs, is a peaceful addition to the community tank.

Red Rasbora *(Trigonostigma heteromorpha)*

Family: Cyprinidae
Distribution: Southeast Asia
Size: 2 inches
Food: Omnivorous
Temperature: 72 to 77 degrees
Fahrenheit

Red Rasboras like to live in groups of eight or more fish.

This popular schooling species requires a group of eight or more fish to be at its best. Because of its size, it should be kept with other equally small and peaceful species. Males are distinguishable from females by a slightly rounded edge at the bottom of the black body marking.

The Red Rasbora is deeper bodied than its close relative, the Red-striped Rasbora *(Rasbora pauciperforata)*, which is more streamlined. This species gets about an inch larger, has similar temperature preferences, and is ideal for the community aquarium when maintained in groups of eight or more. Egglaying species of Rasboras are not as easy to breed as the Barbs, but they are extremely peaceful.

Neon Tetra *(Paracheirodon innesi)*

Family: Characidae
Distribution: Peru
Size: 1.5 inches
Food: Omnivorous
Temperature: 68 to 79 degrees Fahrenheit

In a properly lit tank, Neon Tetras will glow.

Capable of tolerating a wide range of temperatures, this is considered by many to be the most popular of all aquarium fish. Like other midwater fish, the Neon Tetra should be kept in a school of six or more individuals. The iridescent coloration of this fish will glow if the tank is properly lighted. Related species, including the Cardinal Tetra *(Paracheirodon axelrodi)* and the Glowlight Tetra *(Hemigrammus erythrozonus)*, are also peaceful schooling fish that contribute greatly to a community tank. The Black Neon Tetra *(Hyphessobrycon herbertax-elrodi)* has a stouter body than the Neon Tetra and makes an ideal community fish as well. In all these species of Tetra, the males are generally slimmer than the females.

Angelfish *(Pterophyllum scalare)*

Family: Cichlidae
Distribution: From Central Amazon to Peru, and Ecuador
Size: 6 inches
Food: Herbivorous
Temperature: 75 to 82 degrees Fahrenheit

Angelfish cannot tolerate extreme fluctuations in water quality and temperature.

The unique beauty of these fish is very appealing to beginners, but you must have a well-established aquarium with constant water conditions. They cannot tolerate extreme fluctuations in water quality and temperature. Once you establish your aquarium and water quality remains constant, you can introduce this species. These are placid fish that require tall decorations (such as plants) where they will stay quietly. They are best kept in small groups of four to six with other even-tempered fish, such as Neon Tetras and Black Mollies. The Angelfish is one of the few Cichlids that has a somewhat peaceful disposition. However, this species can grow up to 6 inches long and will eat smaller fish at this size. The many varieties of Angelfish come in a wide range of patterns and colors.

Blue Gourami *(Trichogaster trichopterus)*

Family: Osphronemidae
Distribution: From Southeast Asia to the Indo-Australian Islands
Size: 4 inches
Food: Omnivorous
Temperature: 72 to 82 degrees Fahrenheit

Blue Gouramis do well in pairs.

The Blue Gourami and its relatives, the Dwarf Gourami *(Colisa lalia),* the Snakeskin Gourami *(Trichogaster pectoralis),* and the Pearl Gourami *(Trichogaster leerii),* are peaceful labyrinth fish that do not need to be kept in groups but do quite well in pairs. Their elaborate fins and various color forms warrant that care, and they should not be mixed with fin nippers, such as Tiger Barbs. Although listed here as midwater fish, the Gouramis will swim among the bottom decorations and make frequent excursions to the surface. These egglayers build bubblenests during spawning, like other labyrinth fish.

The Paradise Fish *(Macropodus opercularis)* closely resembles the Gouramis and is also a very hardy labyrinth fish that can tolerate temperatures down to 61 degrees Fahrenheit. However, this species may cause trouble, annoying other community species if they are very slow; adult males will frequently fight.

Glass Catfish *(Kryptopterus bicirrhis)*

Family: Siluridae
Distribution: Eastern India and Southeast Asia
Size: 4 inches
Food: Carnivorous
Temperature: 72 to 79 degrees Fahrenheit

Glass Catfish like to swim with at least four of their peers.

This species is one of the few aquarium Catfish that does not inhabit the tank bottom. Like other midwater fish, this schooling species should be placed with at least four of its peers. The Glass Catfish has a transparent body. Although sometimes difficult to acclimate to the aquarium, this hardy fish is a worthwhile addition to a community tank.

Bottom Fish

These fish generally belong to the Catfish group, but there are other species that prefer to stay on or near the bottom. The bottom fish are usually tank cleaners, eating bottom detritus and algae. Therefore, no aquarium would be complete without a few.

Corydoras Catfish *(Corydoras species)*

Family: Callichthyidae
Distribution: South America
Size: 1.5 to 2.5 inches
Food: Omnivorous
Temperature: 72 to 79 degrees Fahrenheit

The Bronze Corydoras tends to be nocturnal.

The Corydoras Catfish are very similar to one another and come in many varieties. They are generally very hardy fish that feed on the substrate with their whiskerlike barbels. Popular species include the Bronze Corydoras *(Corydoras aeneus)*, the Skunk Corydoras *(Corydoras arcuatus)*, the Pink Corydoras *(Corydoras axelrodi)*, the Leopard Corydoras *(Corydoras julii)*, and the Dusky

Corydoras *(Corydoras septentrionalis)*. These fish have a flat bottom so they can stay close to the substrate. They have an adipose fin and armored bony plates rather than scales. They tend to be nocturnal, going about their cleaning business at night. During the day, they like to find a quiet place to hide. They like to live with others of their species, so keep three to five together. Don't depend on the substrate to feed these fish; their diet should be augmented with other foods.

Flying Fox *(Epalzeorhynchos kalopterus)*

Family: Cyprinidae
Distribution: Borneo, Indonesia, Thailand, and India
Size: 6 inches
Food: Omnivorous
Temperature: 75 to 79 degrees Fahrenheit

The Flying Fox is a loner, so just one is enough for your tank.

The Flying Fox is not strictly a bottom species because it rests on the leaves of broad-leafed plants or grazes on the algae on large, flat stones. This species is a loner, so it does not require the company of others of its kind, although a few can be kept in an aquarium if ample space is provided for each to establish its territory.

Clown Loach *(Botia macracanthus)*

Family: Cobitidae
Distribution: Borneo and India
Size: 6 inches
Food: Omnivorous
Temperature: 77 to 86 degrees Fahrenheit

A Clown Loach will help keep the bottom of your tank clean.

This uniquely colorful species of Loach is an excellent addition to any community tank. It has barbels like the Catfish and the same bottom cleaning propensity. It is recommended that you keep several young as a school, but only one mature adult in your aquarium.

Red-tailed Shark
(Epalzeorhynchos bicolor)

Family: Cyprinidae
Distribution: Thailand
Size: 4.5 inches
Food: Omnivorous
Temperature: 72 to 79 degrees
Fahrenheit

Red-tailed Sharks can be aggressive, so it's best to keep only one in your aquarium.

I almost hesitate to include this species in the section on recommended species of tropical fish because of its sometimes aggressive behavior toward other tank fish. It is, however, a very popular community tank fish that is carried by many aquarium supply dealers. It is best to keep a solitary individual in your tank, because these fish occupy territories that they will defend against members of their own species. Only put them together with fast, small fish or with easygoing larger fish.

Clown Plecostomus
(Peckoltia arenaria)

Family: Loricariidae
Distribution: Peru
Size: 4.5 inches
Food: Herbivorous
Temperature: 72 to 80 degrees
Fahrenheit

The Clown Pleco definitely does windows!

It would be difficult to cover the bottom fish without including one of the species of Plecostomus. These fish are famous for their window cleaning abilities. This species is one of the smaller Suckermouthed Catfish and is ideal for a community tank. Others will grow to more than 10 inches long and are not well suited for beginners. This species has been known to be aggressive to its own kind, so it is best to keep only one in your aquarium. Plenty of cover and caves should be provided.

Fish Beginners Should Avoid

There are many fish species that are not well suited to the beginner's aquarium for a number of reasons. Some may be highly sensitive to fluctuating water quality conditions characteristic of the new aquarium. Others may require special water conditions such as softer water or brackish water. The beginner should not try to provide these types of habitats without acquiring some experience. Finally, there are a number of species that are not socially compatible with the peaceful community tank. This group includes large carnivorous fish that eat smaller fish, territorial fish that do not tolerate trespassing, and mature fish that display aggression and combative behavior during spawning or prespawning periods.

Many of these species are offered by aquarium supply stores and may even be promoted by the dealer because the juveniles are considered "harmless." Don't be fooled by this argument; these fish grow fast and develop aggressive attitudes early in life. The small flake-eating baby will become a Tetra-eating carnivore in a matter of months.

Don't be fooled into buying a fish that requires special water conditions. It may live for days or weeks in your tank, but chronic stress will set in, the fish's immune response will fail, and the fish will ultimately die from disease.

As you develop your talents as an aquarist, you will expand your capabilities and be able to keep some of the more sensitive species of fish. You may even want to establish an aquarium of "compatible" aggressive species or a species tank. But start off with fish that are easier to keep and give yourself the opportunity to develop your experience and talents as an aquarist.

The following is a brief description of some species you should avoid in your community aquarium. As you will notice, many of these fish are Cichlids.

Blue Discus *(Symphysodon aequifasciatus)*

Family: Cichlidae
Distribution: Amazon
Size: 6 inches
Food: Carnivorous
Temperature: 79 to 86 degrees Fahrenheit

Blue Discus require soft, acidic water that may not be right for your other fish.

This very peaceful fish would be an attractive addition to a community tank. However, it is best kept in a species aquarium because it requires soft, acidic water and becomes territorial when breeding.

Oscar (Astronotus ocellatus)

Family: Cichlidae
Distribution: South America
Size: 13 inches
Food: Carnivorous
Temperature: 72 to 77 degrees
Fahrenheit

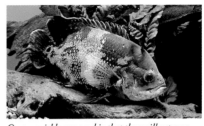

Oscars quickly grow so big that they will eat your other fish.

These undemanding fish are a favorite among aquarists when the fish are young. However, they rapidly grow to a large size and require small fish or meaty food to satisfy their hefty appetites; Goldfish are a common food for domesticated Oscars. They can tolerate a wide range of water quality parameters.

Red Devil (Amphilophus labiatus)

Family: Cichlidae
Distribution: Central America
Size: 10 inches
Food: Omnivorous
Temperature: 75 to 79 degrees
Fahrenheit

The Red Devil is an aggressive fish that will eat just about everything else in your tank.

As the name implies, this Cichlid is an aggressive territorial fish that will eat anything and everything. This species can only be mixed with other species that can take care of themselves.

Jewel Cichlid (Hemichromis bimaculatus)

Family: Cichlidae
Distribution: From Central Liberia to Southern Guinea
Size: 6 inches
Food: Omnivorous
Temperature: 70 to 73 degrees
Fahrenheit

The Jewel Cichlid is especially aggressive when breeding.

The Jewel Cichlid is noted for its extremely aggressive behavior when breeding. This belligerent fish will establish a territory and aggressively protect it.

Jack Dempsey (*Cichlasoma octofasciatum*)

Family: Cichlidae
Distribution: Central America
Size: 8 inches
Food: Omnivorous
Temperature: 72 to 77 degrees Fahrenheit

The Jack Dempsey should be housed only with other large, tough Cichlids.

This is yet another member of the Cichlid family that is intolerant of other species. The Jack Dempsey belongs in a species aquarium; otherwise it will incessantly harass smaller species.

Runny-nose (Firehead) Tetra (*Hemigrammus bleheri*)

Family: Charicidae
Distribution: Colombia and Brazil
Size: 2 inches
Food: Omnivorous
Temperature: 72 to 79 degrees Fahrenheit

The Runny-nose Tetra is highly sensitive to water quality.

This species of Tetra is highly sensitive to water quality conditions. Any buildup of nitrates will cause chronic stress and endanger the fish.

Tinfoil Barb (*Barbonymus schwanenfeldii*)

Family: Cyprinidae
Distribution: Southeast Asia
Size: 14 inches
Food: Omnivorous
Temperature: 72 to 77 degrees Fahrenheit

Tinfoil Barbs tend to grow too big for the average aquarium.

Although they are commonly offered in aquarium supply stores for the community tank, these fish are very active and grow far too large for the average aquarium. They require a lot of space, are best kept in schools, and have a tendency to dig up the substrate.

Sucking Loach (Gyrinocheilus aymonieri)

Family: Gyrinocheilidae
Distribution: India and Thailand
Size: 11 inches
Food: Herbivorous
Temperature: 77 to 82 degrees Fahrenheit

The Sucking Loach grows up to be big and aggressive.

Like most Loaches, this species is an algae eater. However, it can get aggressive toward its tankmates and becomes territorial as it gets larger. Its large size also precludes inclusion in a community tank.

Red Snakehead (Channa micropeltes)

Family: Channidae
Distribution: India, Burma, Thailand, Vietnam, and Malaysia
Size: 39 inches
Food: Carnivorous
Temperature: 77 to 82 degrees Fahrenheit

The Red Snakehead eats small live fish, and can consume your community.

This large carnivore requires warm temperatures and small live fish to feed on. Although juveniles are considered "cute," they grow rapidly and will consume the community.

Mudskipper (Periophthalmus barbarus)

Family: Gobiidae
Distribution: Africa, Southeast Asia, and Australia
Size: 6 inches
Food: Carnivorous
Temperature: 77 to 86 degrees Fahrenheit

This Flagfin Mudskipper needs brackish water, which it must leave periodically.

This fish is becoming increasingly popular in the aquarium trade. However, it requires brackish water, which it needs to leave periodically. Its territorial nature can be a problem as well.

Clown Knifefish (*Chitala chitala*)

Family: Notopteridae
Distribution: Southeast Asia
Size: 39 inches
Food: Omnivorous
Temperature: 75 to 82 degrees
Fahrenheit

The Knifefish gets too big for a typical community tank.

The Knifefish in general gets too large for the average community aquarium. This species and its relatives can be extremely aggressive and are best kept alone or with other large fish.

Arowana (*Osteoglossum bicirrhosum*)

Family: Osteoglossidae
Distribution: Amazon
Size: 47 inches
Food: Carnivorous
Temperature: 75 to 82 degrees
Fahrenheit

This Arowana can grow to almost 4 feet long!

The Arowana is an elegant fish that enchants the novice as well as the expert aquarist. However, its large size and predatory nature exclude it from the community aquarium.

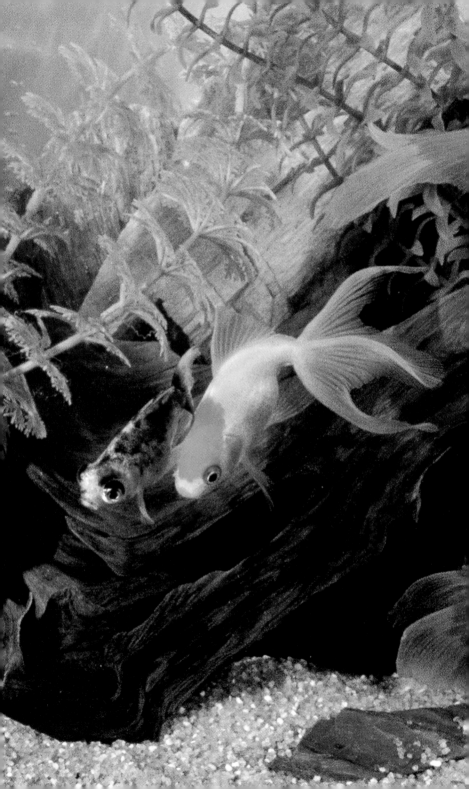

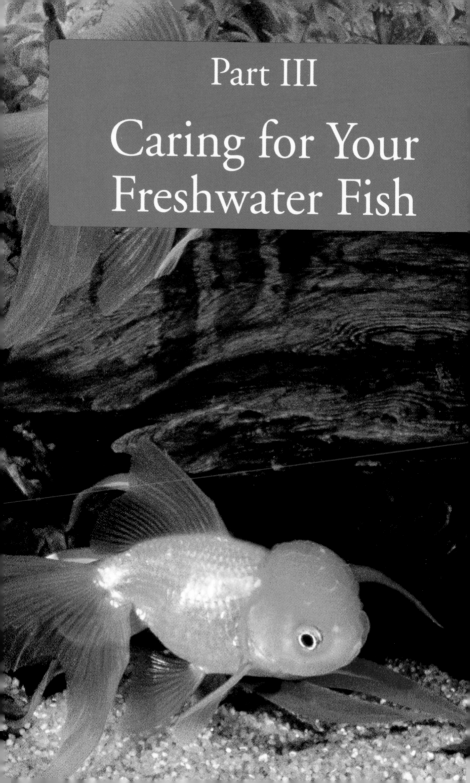

Part III

Caring for Your Freshwater Fish

Chapter 6

Feeding Your Fish

In their natural environment, fish have to find their own food. They hunt, they scavenge, and they graze. In the aquarium, your pets are spoiled. They don't have to work too hard to eat. This puts the responsibility on you to provide them with a well-balanced diet that keeps them alive and healthy.

The raw materials needed for life are called nutrients. Fish, like all other animals, need these nutrients for sustenance, growth, and reproduction. They can only get nutrients from organic matter that has at one time or another been alive.

Feeding Strategies

There are many considerations when it comes to providing food for your fish. In their natural habitat, fish have evolved various feeding strategies to optimize their ability to get nutrients. With all the different kinds of fish and habitats, you can imagine that there are many kinds of feeding strategies. In general, fish can be classified by their feeding strategy into three general groups: carnivores, herbivores, and omnivores.

Carnivores

In their natural habitat, carnivorous fishes feed on other fish or invertebrates that they bite, engulf, or crush. In the aquarium, many tropical fish have been successfully fed dead food, commercially prepared pellets and flakes, or live critters. Pieces of fish, shrimp, and other meats will be taken by most carnivores, but some species will simply not accept anything except live food. Guppies and

Feeding Strategies

Carnivores only eat other fish, invertebrates, and live food. Piranhas, for example, only eat animals.

Herbivores eat only vegetable matter. They will eat flake foods and other types of plant matter, including the plants and algae in your tank. An excellent example of these is the Angelfish.

Most of the fish listed in this book are **omnivores.** They will eat flakes, live foods, and bits of table food. Basically, they will eat almost anything. They are clearly the easiest group to feed and are thus the most highly recommended for beginning aquarists.

Goldfish are commonly offered to these predators. None of the community fish recommended in chapter 5 require live food.

Herbivores

Fishes that prefer to eat vegetation, such as algae and plants, are called herbivores. This can be a problem if you intend to have live plants with herbivorous fish in your aquarium. However, if you feed these fish correctly, they will not wreak havoc on your plant community. Fish that require a diet of this nature will consume commercially prepared vegetable flakes. Their diet can be augmented with some household vegetables, including peas, lettuce, green beans, and cauliflower. It is also important to have a lush growth of algae in your aquarium if you intend to house herbivorous fish.

Omnivores

If a species of fish is not selective about whether it eats meat or vegetable matter, it is an omnivore. These fish will feed on a variety of foods and have no specific dietary preferences. Many of the species recommended in chapter 5 are considered omnivorous. A new hobbyist should not have to worry about special feeding strategies when setting up an aquarium for the first time. Although these fish will accept commercially prepared flake and pellet foods, providing a good variety of foods is necessary to meet all their dietary requirements.

Most of the fish recommended for a beginner aquarist are omnivores, like this Guppy.

Types of Fish Foods

There are many different types of food for your freshwater tropical fish. Carnivores will eat flake food, brine shrimp, and almost any kind of seafood—crab, lobster, oysters, and clams. Herbivores will adapt to an omnivorous diet, taking flake and frozen foods as well as vegetables, while grazing on aquarium algae. Omnivores will eat all of these foods.

Aquarium foods can be grouped into a variety of categories, and different experts do it differently. I prefer to classify aquarium foods into three general categories: natural foods, prepared foods, and live foods.

Natural Foods

This group of foods includes items that are obtained fresh, frozen, or freeze-dried. They are not heavily processed. They can be fed to the fish fresh, cooked, or dried. Foods in this category include leafy green vegetables, fish and invertebrate flesh, and frozen or freeze-dried invertebrates.

Leafy Greens

For herbivores, it is essential to provide some vegetable matter. While the algae in your aquarium may be enough for some grazing fishes, you should also feed vegetables that are fresh, blanched, or thawed after freezing. Common vegetables that are good for fish include lettuce, spinach, cabbage, parsley, kale, and water-cress. Some aquarists prefer that you blanch the vegetables to aid in their digestion. This means they are boiled for just a minute or two to soften them up and break down cell membranes. They must then be cooled to room temperature before you offer them to your fish.

In general, vegetables are composed mostly of water and are low in energy, protein, and fats, but contain high concentrations of carbohydrates, fiber, and certain vitamins. You do not want to feed your fish vegetables exclusively, but be prepared to provide some to your herbivorous fish.

Meaty Foods

This category includes a variety of foods made of fish and invertebrate meats. They are fed fresh, thawed, or cooked. Cooking these foods does not lower their nutritional value. Cooking is also a good idea because raw seafood can carry infectious disease that can be transmitted to aquarium fish. Cooking can involve boiling, steaming, or using foods that are canned in water, which are already boiled.

The variety of meats available is vast. This category includes fishes such as herring, anchovy, smelt, mackerel, and tuna, as well as shellfish such as clams, shrimp, mussels, scallops, oysters, crabs, and squid. In general, meaty foods contain less

Carnivorous fishes need meaty foods. You need not sacrifice a Goldfish to accomplish this; they can eat cooked seafood.

Household Foods for Your Fish

Frozen (serve thawed): clams, oysters, lobster, crab, shrimp, fish, and mussels

Canned: the same as frozen, plus green beans and peas

Raw: the same as frozen, plus spinach and lettuce

Cooked: green beans, peas, broccoli, and cauliflower

Live food and foods other than flakes are highly desirable additions to your fish's diets, but remember to feed pellets or flakes as a staple. If you feed your fish household food, always serve it plain, not seasoned, salted, or spiced.

water and carbohydrates and substantially more protein and fats than does vegetable matter. It is very important that you include this type of food for carnivorous fishes.

Frozen and Freeze-dried Foods

These foods often provide the greatest portion of your fish's diet, because many are specifically produced for aquariums and they are widely available. The dietary value of these foods is similar to that of meaty foods. Some of the most common commercially available frozen foods in this category include brine shrimp, plankton, krill, and other shrimps. Also, many of the seafoods that I mentioned above are offered frozen, such as fish, squid, scallops, shrimp, and clams.

Frozen foods are generally packaged in such a way that you can break off a chunk and put it in the aquarium. I prefer to thaw the food first in a small cup of water from the tank, then pour the mixture into the aquarium.

Freeze-drying has made it possible to preserve a variety of natural foods for aquarium fish. For the marine (saltwater) aquarium, the process has most often been applied to brine shrimp and other small invertebrates such as krill, tubifex worms, and bloodworms. These critters can also be fed to freshwater fish. They are not processed and what you see is what you get—the whole animal without water.

These foods will help increase the variety of what you are feeding your fish, but they should not be the only food offered. While it has been shown that freeze-dried brine shrimp have the same fat concentrations as freshly killed brine shrimp, it has not been proven that they are a complete dietary substitute for live brine shrimp.

Prepared Foods

This category of food includes the flake and dry foods that are commercially processed for aquarium fish, but may also include frozen processed foods that contain a number of healthy ingredients. Prepared foods try to approximate in ideal amounts the three basic requirements of proteins, fats, and carbohydrates. They are also supplemented with vitamins and minerals.

These foods come in many varieties depending on the type of fish (carnivore, herbivore, or omnivore), and new formulations are being added every year to better meet the dietary needs of your pets. Even algae that are dried in sheets are becoming a popular dried food for fishes.

Prepared foods come in many forms, depending on the size or feeding behavior of the fish. Flakes, tablets, pellets, and crumb forms are available. For example, larger predatory fishes should be fed pellets as opposed to flakes, because they prefer to consume a large morsel. In addition, fish that feed on the bottom may not venture to the surface for flakes, so they must be fed pellets or tablets that sink to the bottom. Pellets can be stuck to the aquarium glass, as well, for the grazing species in your tank.

Prepared foods come in many forms and are nutritionally balanced. They are great as a staple, but your fish will be healthier if you supplement their diets with other foods.

Many of the fish mentioned in this book can be fed prepared foods. However, if you want active, colorful, and healthy fish, you must vary their diets. Flakes are good as a staple food, but you should make every effort to substitute other foods daily to enrich your fish.

Live Foods

Live food is an excellent source of nutrition for the fish in your aquarium. Fishes and invertebrates that are fed live foods ordinarily grow faster, and have vibrant colors and higher survival rates. This is because live foods retain active enzymes

How to Feed Your Fish

By far the biggest problem for new aquarists when feeding fish is determining how much and how often to feed them. Some fish are gluttons, while others will stop when they have had enough. In general, many experts feel it is better to feed too little than too much. Follow the guidelines below when feeding your fish and you will develop a working sense of how much and how often to feed them.

1. Offer as much food as your fish will eat in five minutes. Flakes should sink no deeper than one-third the height of the tank. Provide tablets or pellets for bottom fish.
2. Feed your fish in very small portions over the five-minute period.
3. If you are home during the day, feed your fish over the course of the day in small portions. If you are not home during the day, feed your fish twice a day at the same times every day—once in the morning and once at night.
4. Always feed your fish at the same spot in the tank.
5. Don't overfeed the fish, no matter how much you think they need more food. Overeating will stress your fish and cause detritus and uneaten food to accumulate in the tank, degrading water quality.

Watch all your fish during feeding, making sure that each gets its share of food. Remember that fish have different mouth shapes that enable them to feed at different levels in the tank. Some species will not go to the surface to eat, and will wait for food to disperse throughout the tank. Don't rely on surface feedings and the leftovers of others to feed bottom fish. Pellets that sink to the bottom should be provided for these fish. Remember, refusal to eat is one of the first signs of illness, so keep an eye out for fish that seem to have no interest in food.

Try not to feed your fish right after turning on the light; they won't be fully alert until about thirty minutes later. In addition, don't crumble the flake food. This will add fine particles to the water that are not ingested, thereby degrading water quality. Your fish won't have any problems biting and grinding whole flake food.

If you are going to be away from your aquarium for up to a few days, the fish will be fine without food. For extended periods, make arrangements for someone to feed your fish or install an automatic food dispenser. If you choose the latter, be sure not to overload the dispenser, and set a long interval between feeding times so the fish will eat all that is offered.

that make digestion more efficient. Also, there are very few fish species that won't eat live foods, so this is the best way to get the picky eaters to eat.

It is generally thought that live foods are an essential requirement of captive fishes and that they must be included as a dietary supplement. The type of live food you give your pets depends on the size of the fish you are feeding. The most common live foods you will find at your dealer are:

- **Feeder fish:** Small freshwater fishes, including Guppies and Goldfish, are popular food items for larger predatory fish like Oscars.

- **Earthworms:** These backyard dirt dwellers offer an economical food source for many of your aquarium fish. They can be served whole or in pieces, depending on the size of your fish. Be sure to rinse them thoroughly.

Varying your fish's diet by including live food like this earthworm will result in more active, colorful fish.

- **Blackworms and tubifex worms:** Many dealers carry these freshwater worms that are readily consumed by aquarium fishes. These live worms make an excellent addition to your fish's diet. Before feeding them to your fish, you must rinse them thoroughly.

- **Daphnia:** Also referred to as water fleas, these constitute another excellent live food for your fish. Daphnia should only be fed to your fish every now and then because they can cause digestive problems.

- **Drosophila:** These are the larvae of the wingless fruit fly. Like the other live foods, you can sometimes buy them from the aquarium supply store.

- **Bloodworms:** Also known as two-winged fly larvae, these are usually in good supply year-round and can be purchased at your aquarium supply store.

Brine Shrimp

The most popular live food for tropical marine fish is brine shrimp, and they can also be fed to freshwater species. The brine shrimp (*Artemia* species) is a primitive crustacean inhabiting salt pans in more than 160 locations around the world. Those in your local aquarium supply store probably originated in San

Make sure that you do not overfeed your fish. The portions may look small, but they are very small animals.

Francisco Bay or Great Salt Bay in Utah. They are one of the best sources of nutrition available for aquarium organisms of any type.

Brine shrimp are an excellent source of fat and protein. Of all the live food available, they are the safest because they do not carry disease. An added advantage is that you can raise them yourself, because many dealers offer brine shrimp eggs. It is best to follow the instructions accompanying the eggs.

Chapter 7

Maintaining Your Aquarium

You planned your aquarium, bought your equipment, set up your tank, established excellent water quality, carefully selected and introduced the fish, and fed them well. Now it's time to learn how to maintain the quality of their new home. Aquarium maintenance involves everything from turning the light on and off every day, to feeding the fish, to spending time observing them. This last task is certainly the most enjoyable. Get to know your fish, watch how they interact and make note of any unusual behavior. Closely check the fish for any signs of disease and watch their interactions to see if any are being picked on. If you have live plants, check them to see if any parts are brown or dying. If they are, remove these sections at once.

The more stable you make the conditions in your aquarium, the less likely you are to stress your fish. Rapid or frequent fluctuations in water temperature and water quality cause stress and therefore compromise the health of your fish. You must monitor the water temperature, making sure it remains constant. Examine the filter, the heater, and the airstones to make sure they are in good working order. The filter may have a blockage, especially if you are using a box filter. The thermostat light in the heater should be working properly. Make sure the air pump and airstones are operating at maximum efficiency. These things should be checked daily or weekly, and require just a few minutes of your time.

While you are feeding or simply enjoying your pets, you can perform a routine check of the tank components and the aquarium occupants.

General Maintenance

Cleaning an aquarium involves an active, conscientious effort on your part. Maintaining a fish tank is not for the lazy. Don't set up a tank if you don't intend to follow through and keep it clean and healthy. All too often, interest wanes after the first couple of months and your aquarium fish ultimately suffer the consequences of poor water quality. Realize that going into this hobby requires a real commitment on your part. Concern must be shown at every step and on every level. Your fish's lives depend on your attention to detail.

Vacuuming

Vacuuming is one of the most important steps in maintaining your aquarium. You must prevent detritus from accumulating in the gravel. Detritus is the combination of fish wastes, plant fragments, and uneaten food that ends up on the

If you do not regularly maintain your tank, your fish will definitely suffer.

bottom of the aquarium and decays. If it is not removed, this organic waste ultimately breaks down into ammonia, which disturbs your water chemistry and can harm your fish. If detritus is allowed to accumulate to excessive levels, your filter clogs and water quality goes downhill fast. If you have an undergravel filter, vacuuming is still very important because too much waste will clog these filters, preventing water flow through the gravel.

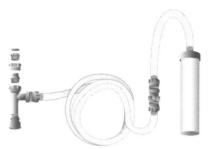

You can buy a gravel vacuum that both siphons and refills the tank.

Aquarium vacuums or substrate cleaners are available from your aquarium supply dealer. You can also use a simple hose to siphon wastes while you are doing a water change. This accomplishes two goals at once: vacuuming detritus and removing water from the tank.

Check the Filter

No matter what kind of filter you have, it is important to regularly examine the filter media. With most box and power filters, the top-level filter media mat gets dirty quickly and easily, as this is the level that collects the largest pieces of debris. The excessive accumulation of detritus in your filter inhibits flow and ultimately reduces the filter's effectiveness.

Rinse the filter media every three or four weeks under lukewarm water until the water is clear. You should probably replace about 50 percent of the media every month, making sure to re-use about half of the old filter material. This way, the viable working bacterial colony in your filter medium will not be thrown out and you won't have to start from square one. One of the most common mistakes is to replace the entire filter contents because it looks dirty. Some of that "dirt" is bacteria that are beneficial to the filtering process. For filters that use cartridges as media, check with the manufacturer for optimum maintenance and replacement rate.

Control Algae

Algae are relatively simple photosynthetic organisms that range in size from the one-celled microscopic types to large seaweeds that grow to over 230 feet. Algae are also very hardy organisms that have a tremendous reproductive capacity.

Your filter is only as clean as the filter media. Check and replace the filter media regularly.

They can enter your aquarium as algal spores borne by the air or carried by tank furnishings from another aquarium.

Algae Everywhere

Algae are organisms that occur throughout the world in many habitats, ranging from freshwater to saltwater, and from the Arctic to the equator. For many years, algae were grouped with the fungi into the class of plants known as *Thallophyta*. More recently, scientists have classified these plantlike organisms into their own kingdom, called *Protoctista*.

Algae have adapted to all kinds of water conditions. In your aquarium, they can be found on the surface, suspended in the water, or on the surfaces of rocks, gravel, and tank decorations. At low levels, algae can be somewhat beneficial to the aquarium, providing the same benefits as plants. Like plants, algae are photosynthetic so they convert carbon dioxide into oxygen. The reduction of carbon dioxide in your aquarium is a good thing. In addition, algae act as convenient organisms that can be used to remove excess nutrients from your aquarium. By routinely scraping some of your algae from the tank, you will be physically getting nitrates, phosphates, and other nutrients out of your aquarium. Algae also provide food for herbivorous fish.

However, when algae are present, they generally grow in excess if the right conditions exist. Excessive algal growth overruns a tank unless water quality is properly maintained. High nitrate levels and sunlight promote algal growth. Avoiding these conditions minimizes algae as a tank nuisance.

If you have excessive algal growth, there are several measures you can take to reduce the presence of algae in your aquarium.

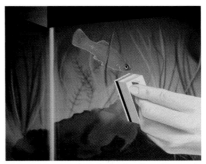

It is important to clean the surface film of dirt and algae from the inside of your tank. A magnetic scraper is one way to do that.

- Introduce algae eaters such as Flying Foxes, Black Mollies, and Corydoras Catfish to keep algae in check on gravel, rocks, and plants.
- Keep the aquarium well planted; nitrates will be consumed by healthy aquarium plants instead of being available for algae.
- Reduce the duration of light to ten hours per day instead of twelve hours.
- Make sure that all rocks, plants, decorations, and gravel going into the tank are free of algae.
- Scrape algae from the aquarium walls with an algae scraper. These are either sponges attached to a long stick, a razor blade attached to a stick, or magnetic scrapers.
- Remove excess nitrates, which fuel algal growth, by doing partial water changes in a timely fashion.

Don't become obsessed with algae to the point where you feel that all algae must be removed from the aquarium. I guarantee you this is simply something that can't be effectively done. Expect to live with some algae in your tank.

Test the Water

When you first set up the aquarium, testing the water every couple of days is critical to the water maturation process. As you begin to add fish, water chemistry changes radically and water quality monitoring is critical to the survival of your fish. After this sensitive period of two to four weeks, it is still very important to test your water, and I recommend that you do so every week for the first two months. This gives you a good understanding of the mechanics of the nitrogen cycle. Water testing also tells you when the nitrates have risen to the point where a water change is needed.

After two months, your tank will be well established and the need to test the water every week diminishes. At this point, a monthly water test will suffice unless you suspect you might have tank problems. Sudden behavioral changes in your fish, fish disease, fish mortality, excessive algal growth, smelly water, and cloudy water all warrant an immediate water quality test and a possible water change.

Partial Water Changes

> **TIP**
>
> **A Quarantine Tank**
>
> To evaluate the health of their new fish, serious aquarists establish a quarantine tank. A quarantine tank is a much smaller and simpler aquarium set up for that purpose. The quarantine tank needs to be properly filtered and tested routinely, just like the main aquarium. As a beginner, you shouldn't need such a tank if you buy hardy fish from a reputable dealer.

Partial water changes are one of the most important aspects of maintaining your aquarium. During a partial water change, you take out a percentage of the aquarium water and replace it with fresh or distilled water. The amount you change varies with the quality of your tank and with the frequency of water changes. Some experts believe a 10 percent water change is sufficient every week, while others think it should be closer to 20 percent. I recommend that you start with a water change of 10 to 20 percent every week, and raise or lower this amount depending on your water quality.

Partial water changes help maintain good water quality because you are diluting the amount of nitrogenous compounds such as nitrites and nitrates, harmful gases, and other toxic substances each time you change the water. The water you add, which should be pure distilled water if possible, is more oxygen rich than the water in your tank.

The best time to do a partial water change is while you are vacuuming your tank. Otherwise, you can use a siphon and a large bucket. The siphon is basically just a 3- or 4-foot hose or tube that will transfer water from the tank to the bucket.

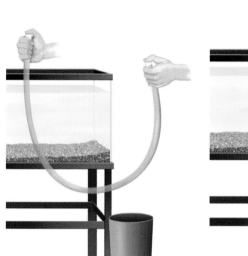

Fill the siphon with water and use your thumbs to block both ends.

Place one end in the tank and one end in the bucket, and water will flow.

How to Siphon

1. Fill the siphon tube completely with water, making sure there is no trapped air anywhere in the tube. Make sure the siphon is clean and your hands are clean as well. You can fill the hose at the sink or by submerging it in the aquarium. Only do the latter if your aquarium is large enough to accommodate the tube without spooking the fish. Use your thumbs to block both ends of the siphon to keep the water in and the air out.

2. Keeping your thumbs in place, place one end of the tube in the aquarium and aim the other at the bucket. Make sure the bucket end is lower than the aquarium or siphoning will not work. If you filled your siphon in the aquarium, plug one end of the tube tightly, lift it from the aquarium and lower it to the bucket.

3. Release your thumbs and the water will begin to flow rapidly from the aquarium into the bucket.

Just like the aquarium vacuum, the siphon can be used to remove debris from the tank while you are making a water change. When it is time to add water, if distilled water is not available, use tap water that you have allowed to age for one

Your fish, even the bottom-feeders and algae-eaters like this one, cannot keep the tank clean themselves.
You must do it for them.

or two days. Keep a few 1-gallon jugs or a 5-gallon bucket filled with water available so it's on hand whenever you need it. Make sure the temperature of the water you add is close to that of the aquarium water.

Maintenance Checklist

Daily

- ❑ Feed the fish twice a day.
- ❑ Turn the tank lights on and off.
- ❑ Check the water temperature.
- ❑ Check the heater and make sure the thermostat light is working.
- ❑ Make sure the filter is working properly.
- ❑ Make sure the aerator is working properly.

Weekly

- ❑ Study the fish closely, watching for behavioral changes and signs of disease.
- ❑ Change approximately 10 to 20 percent of the aquarium water.

❑ Add distilled or aged water to compensate for water evaporation.
❑ Check the filter to see if the top mat needs to be replaced.
❑ Vacuum the tank thoroughly and attempt to clean detritus.
❑ Test the water for pH, nitrates, and softness (first two months).
❑ Trim and fertilize aquarium plants as needed.

Monthly

❑ Change 25 percent of the aquarium water.
❑ Clean the tank's inside glass with an algae scraper.
❑ Vacuum the tank thoroughly, stirring up the gravel and eliminating detritus.
❑ Test the water for pH, nitrates, and softness.
❑ Rinse any tank decorations that have dirt and algae buildup.
❑ Trim and fertilize plants; replace plants if necessary.

Quarterly

❑ Change 50 percent of the water; replace with distilled or aged water.
❑ Replace airstones.
❑ Rinse the filter materials completely and replace some of them if necessary.
❑ Vacuum the tank thoroughly, stirring up the gravel and eliminating detritus and debris.
❑ Trim and fertilize plants as needed; replace if necessary.
❑ Test the water for pH, nitrates, and softness.
❑ Rinse any tank decorations that have dirt and algae buildup.

Yearly

❑ Strip down the filter; replace at least 50 percent of the media with a new mat and charcoal.
❑ Replace the airstones.
❑ Wash all the gravel.
❑ Empty the tank (save some of the original aquarium water to help condition the tank) and clean the inside thoroughly.
❑ Restart the aquarium all over again.

Chapter 8

Keeping Your Fish Healthy

Freshwater fish are subject to all kinds of maladies. Nasty pathogens that cause disease are in and around your fish in their natural setting and in your aquarium. These pathogens may be bacterial, viral, fungal, or parasitic. Many are introduced with new fish and many are highly contagious.

Fortunately, many of the diseases caused by these agents will manifest themselves with signs that are easy to recognize. Unfortunately, there are not a lot of treatments available for the home aquarist, and there are no guarantees that your aquarium fish will be saved.

Whether or not disease breaks out depends on the resistance of your fish. Poor living conditions weaken your fish, cause chronic stress, and ultimately compromise the fish's immune systems. This is why I have repeatedly stressed the importance of maintaining a healthy aquarium for your pets. Even if you do everything in your power to maintain a disease-free aquarium, you may have to confront health problems in your fish; even experts fall victim to these problems.

Signs of Illness

The first step to treating any kind of ailment in your aquarium is to recognize and identify the problem. You can determine if a fish is not healthy by its appearance and its behavior. Since you have been spending time examining your fish while you feed them, you should be able to identify problems as soon as they develop.

If anything looks abnormal on any part of a fish's body, suspect disease. This is a Varu Cichlid.

Telltale behavioral signs of illness include:

- Lack of appetite
- Hyperventilation of the gills
- Gasping for air near the surface
- Erratic swimming behavior
- Lack of movement
- Rubbing the body or fins against objects in the tank
- Twitching fins

External symptoms include a variety of physical abnormalities of the head, body, fins, gills, scales, and anal vent. The key to diagnosing the various diseases associated with aquarium fish is to learn the symptoms of each one.

Treatments

It is very important that beginners use commercially available treatments instead of homemade remedies. Some experts recommend chemicals such as malachite green or potassium permanganate. These chemicals must be handled in very exact dosages. If a fish is overdosed with one of them, it can kill the fish faster than the disease.

Discuss all the possible remedies for a disease with your local aquarium supply dealer. If you are still not satisfied, don't be afraid to call your veterinarian and ask a few questions. If your veterinarian does not treat fish, he can usually recommend someone who does. Finally, when you apply the remedy, make sure you follow the directions *exactly.*

The Old-fashioned Salt Bath

This is the most time-tested cure-all of the freshwater fish world. Sometimes called the progressive saltwater treatment, it is how the hospital tank (see the box on page 101) is most often used. This very simple treatment has been known to cure a number of fish diseases, including ich, fungus, velvet, and tail rot. Many experts swear by it.

You simply add 1 teaspoon of table salt (not iodized) for each gallon of water to the hospital tank that houses your sick fish. Add the same amount of salt that night and twice the next day, again in the morning and at night. If there is no improvement by the third or fourth day, add 1 more teaspoon of salt each day. On the ninth and tenth days, make progressive water changes and check for results.

Sometimes the best thing to do is empty and scrub the tank and start your fish out in a new, clean environment.

Emergency Cleaning

If any of the infestations mentioned below strike more than three or four fish, you need to take drastic measures and perform an emergency cleaning. This is the most extreme treatment for disease in your aquarium. Place all the fish in the hospital tank and begin treatment. Then turn your attention to the aquarium.

This very simply involves thoroughly cleaning your aquarium and starting it up again from scratch. Throw out filter media and empty out the contents of the tank. Wash the walls, the gravel, and the filter with bleach. Of course, make sure you rinse everything thoroughly. Then rinse it all again. Do the same with the plastic plants. Throw out the rocks and buy new ones. If you have any live plants, dispose of them too. Replace the filter media and airstones, any tubing, and whatever else you have in the tank. Take the heater and wash it with bleach as well, making sure to rinse it thoroughly. In essence, you are starting over again because your tank was overrun by disease.

Common Diseases

There are literally hundreds of maladies that can afflict fish. Some are specific to certain species and some can easily be transferred between species. Not all are common in the average home aquarium. The following provides a general overview of the diseases you are most likely to encounter in your aquarium. For a more complete listing of tropical fish diseases and their treatments, consult the references in the appendix.

Constipation or Indigestion (not contagious)

A fish that is constipated or suffering from indigestion is often very inactive and usually rests on the bottom of the tank. Its abdomen generally swells or bulges. This can be caused by an incorrect diet, food that doesn't agree with the fish, or overfeeding. You will need to change the food you are feeding this fish.

Isolate the fish in a hospital tank (see the box on page 101). Don't feed the fish for three to five days, until it returns to being active. When it resumes normal behavior, feed it live or freeze-dried food for one week. After one week, return the fish to its normal tank. This is a problem that tends to recur, so make it a point to watch this fish.

Swim bladder disease can result from bruising during fighting or breeding. These two Firemouth Cichlids could be at risk, as they are actually having a heated dispute.

Swim Bladder Problems (not contagious)

This is a fairly easy disease to diagnose, because an affected fish can't swim properly. It suffers from a loss of balance, swimming on its side or upside down, sometimes somersaulting through the water. Swim bladder disease can result from constipation; from bruising of the swim bladder during handling, fighting, or breeding; or from bacterial infection associated with poor water quality.

These problems have been known to correct themselves as the bruised area heals, but you can't always count on this.

If you suspect a bacterial infection, improve water quality and treat the fish with a broad-spectrum antibiotic. If the problem is associated with constipation, your fish is more likely to experience a recurrence. Feed your fish something else, as diet can be one of the biggest reasons this disease develops.

> **TIP**
>
> **Choosing Medications**
>
> Special foods that incorporate medicine, medicated water treatments, and antiseptics are all available at your aquarium supply store to treat a variety of ailments. Because what is available and which medications are best for which illnesses changes over time, it's best to talk to your aquarium supply dealer about what to buy for your fish.

The Hospital Tank

Many experts recommend that you set up a hospital tank to isolate individuals that are suffering from disease. This tank reduces the likelihood the disease will spread to others in the aquarium. It also provides refuge to an ailing fish that may be harassed by healthier fish. The hospital tank makes it easier to treat the fish without subjecting other fish to the treatment, as well. Moreover, it makes it easier for you to observe and diagnose the ailing fish.

As your expertise in this hobby increases over time, it is likely that you will keep expensive fish that you simply do not want to lose to disease. At that point, a hospital tank is mandatory. The hospital tank need not be large; a 10-gallon tank will do. It does need adequate filtration and aeration, but plants and gravel should be left out. Try to provide some kind of cover for the fish in the form of rocks or empty flowerpots as a source of security.

Dropsy or Kidney Bloat (may be contagious)

This is also known as pinecone disease because the belly bloats noticeably and the scales stick out like a pinecone. In general, this disease causes the body to swell due to a buildup of fluid in the tissues. This malady is thought to be caused by water quality problems or some kind of organ failure.

Fish generally don't live more than a week after full-blown dropsy is manifested. Like constipation and swim bladder disease, fish that survive dropsy tend to have recurring attacks. While dropsy is not thought to be contagious, it is best to remove the fish at once.

Many experts still think dropsy is not treatable and that the fish should be immediately removed and painlessly destroyed. Others believe medicated food is one way to treat dropsy. If your fish does not respond to treatment in two or three days, it should probably be humanely destroyed.

Tumors (usually not contagious)

Obvious lumps, bumps, or protrusions, tumors sometimes look like large blisters or warts. They have been known to grow to the size of a large screw head. They can be surgically removed, but only by a veterinarian.

Pop-Eye (not contagious)

This disease, also known as exophthalmus, causes the eyes to bulge from their sockets and is, therefore, easy to recognize in most tropical fish. The condition is generally caused by poor water quality and subsequent chronic stress. Recovery may take several days if efforts are made to improve water quality. Some experts think food should be withheld for two or three days until tank conditions are corrected.

Bacterial, Viral, and Fungal Infections

Furunculosis (contagious)

This bacterial infection goes unnoticed for some time, but then it spreads rapidly. These bacteria infect the flesh under the scales, somewhat like skin flukes (see page 108). This infection is first manifested by the appearance of bumps under the scales. A short time later, the bumps rupture and create large, bleeding ulcers. That is why this ailment is sometimes referred to as ulcer disease. There is no certain cure.

While some fish have actually survived, large scars resulting from the infection often prove to be a problem. Fish with these kinds of ulcers should probably be destroyed.

Ulcers (highly contagious)

This is an infection that tends to begin internally, then manifests itself as large red ulcers, boils, and dark reddening at the bases of the fins. It cannot be mistaken for anchor worm (see page 107) because anchor-worm ulcers swell up, whereas these tend to eat away into the body. That is why this ailment is sometimes referred to as hole-in-the-body disease.

A salt bath may be too harsh, but the infected fish should be isolated immediately and fed medicated food. At times, antibiotics are required and a veterinarian may be required. Consult your local aquarium supply store before proceeding.

If you can, isolate a contagious fish in a separate hospital tank. This is a Marlier's Julie.

Fungus (highly contagious)

The most common species of fungus infecting tropical fish is *Saprolegnia.* It is a fuzzy growth that differs from velvet (see page 109) because it is whiter and easier to notice. The primary cause of this infection is damage to the mucous layer of the skin. This allows fungal spores to germinate and grow into the skin. Injury, environmental conditions, and parasites can damage the protective mucous layer. Commercial remedies are available and the entire aquarium should be treated with a fungicide.

Body Slime Fungus (highly contagious)

This deadly affliction can kill your fish in two days if not caught in time. The protective mucous coating grows white and starts peeling off as if the fish were shedding its skin. The fins are gradually covered as well. Eventually, the body becomes red with irritation.

Do not hesitate to call your aquarium supply store immediately. Commercial remedies are available, but must be administered quickly. A salt bath with warm temperatures may be a temporary solution, as it should retard growth of the fungus. However, a salt bath won't cure the fish, though some have found that severe salt treatments combined with ich (see page 109) cures are effective.

Mouth Fungus (contagious)

This malady, also called Columnaris disease, is caused by the bacteria *Flexibacter* and manifests itself as a white cottony growth on the mouth. It can infect the gills, back, and fins. If left untreated for any length of time, this infection will destroy the entire infected region and lead to eventual death.

Commercial cures are available, but you can begin by isolating the fish and administering the salt treatment. Some aquarists will start with a salt bath and then use a general fungal or bacterial control agent. Consult with your aquarium supply store once you have diagnosed the problem.

Fish Pox (probably not contagious)

This disease affects Goldfish, Koi, and Carp more than it does other aquarium fish, but is still worth mentioning. This is a viral infection that causes milky white or pinkish gray waxy film to develop over the fish's skin and fins. The infection usually appears, gets worse, and then disappears.

It is not definitely known what triggers fish pox, but it does not appear to be contagious. Nonetheless, take the necessary precautions and isolate the infected fish until the film goes away. This will generally take seven to ten days. This ailment is more annoying than anything else, since it does not kill the fish. However, there is no known cure.

Goldfish are more often affected by fish pox.

Fighting and fin nipping are the likely causes of fin rot. This is a Zebra Cichlid.

Fin or Tail Rot (contagious)

This is sometimes caused by fighting among your fish—the fins get damaged and bacteria then infect the injured area. It can also be triggered by poor water quality. It is easily detectable, as the fins have missing parts and eventually become shredded. As the disease worsens, the entire fin will be eaten away. There are many broad-spectrum medications that will help you deal with this situation. Consult your local aquarium supply store dealer.

Be sure to treat the aquarium water as well, because fin rot is usually contagious. Also, take the necessary steps to remedy the cause of the infection. Separate fish that cause injury to the fins and make sure water quality is at its best.

China Disease (highly contagious)

This is not a very common disease, and you must be absolutely certain of your diagnosis. This is the most contagious disease listed here, and the most deadly. There is no known cure for China disease.

The symptoms are very easy to diagnose. The tail fin and other fins begin to fray, very much as in fin rot. However, with China disease it begins at the base of the fin and works its way outward. Also, the infected areas begin to blacken and even the ventral region turns black. Unfortunately, the infected fish must be painlessly destroyed and the other fish put in the hospital tank. A ten-day progressive salt treatment for the remaining fish is a good idea.

In the meantime, you need to perform an emergency cleaning in the tank. This must be done immediately to prevent further damage by this disease.

Parasite Infestations

Fish Lice (highly contagious)

Fish lice are parasitic crustaceans of the species *Argulus* that are very easy to recognize on the surface of your fish. They are round, disk-shaped crustaceans with prominent eyes, sucking disks, and a stiletto mouthpart that clamps firmly onto its host. They can move about the host with ease and tend to take on the color of the fish that they parasitize.

Often the infected fish will rub against objects in the tank in an effort to scrape these pests off. Some fish have been known to jump out of the water in an attempt to cleanse themselves of these parasites. These creatures feed by sucking the blood and tissue fluids out of the fish through the skin and scales. Sometimes they occur on the fins, but this is not as satisfying for them. Fish lice

All parasites are highly contagious and must be dealt with promptly. This is a Skunk Corydoras.

can also transmit other microscopic diseases, and wounds may develop secondary bacterial infections.

Lice are treatable, but both the fish and the aquarium must be treated. There are a number of high-quality commercially produced products to control parasites. Your local aquarium supply dealer can help you to select one. The fish should be quarantined and the tank disinfected with the same parasite control product. On larger fish, experts have been known to remove fish lice with forceps or by dripping hot paraffin wax from a candle onto the parasite. Treat the infected area with an antiseptic after removing the parasite.

Anchor Worm (highly contagious)

These elongated crustaceans of the genus *Lernaea* also attach to the skin of the fish. Several species of this parasite have been described, but all females have a head with an anchor shape that embeds in the flesh of the host. The fish will rub against anything in an attempt to scrape off the parasite. Like fish lice, these creatures cause irritation and localized bleeding at the point of attachment; from this protrudes a white worm that can sometimes grow quite long. Secondary bacterial infection can occur at these points.

Treatment of the anchor worm includes taking the fish out of the water and removing the worm with forceps or tweezers. To remove the worm, place a wet cloth in your hand. Take hold of the fish in the hand holding the cloth. Make sure to position the fish so that the worm is facing you. With a pair of household tweezers, press as close to the ulcer as possible, but only extract the worm. Make sure not to rip any flesh off the fish and be careful not to break the parasite. This is very dangerous to the fish, and you must be extremely cautious when attempting this procedure. It may be best to get someone experienced to do it for you.

Be sure to treat the infected area with an antiseptic after removing the parasite. In addition, antibiotic treatment may accelerate the healing of lesions. Consult your aquarium dealer for a general full-spectrum antibiotic.

Leeches (highly contagious)

Leeches are another group of parasites that may be found on the skin and scales of your fish. These are not the leeches we see as free-living creatures in lakes and ponds. Rather, these are parasitic, wormlike creatures that attach to your fish, feeding on flesh and blood. They need to be removed as quickly as possible, but not with forceps or tweezers. These parasites are very strong, and you are likely to do more damage to your fish than to the leeches by trying to pull them off. Call your aquarium supply store for advice about commercially produced cures.

Your aquarium supply dealer can help you select medications to deal with your fish's illness. This is a Dubois' Cichlid.

Another solution involves preparing a salt bath with 8 teaspoons of salt to each gallon of water. Once the salt is dissolved, add the fish for no more than ten minutes. The leeches that do not fall off can be removed very easily with tweezers. Again, the aquarium needs to be treated immediately with commercially produced chemicals for parasite control. Check all your fish for parasites when one is discovered, and always isolate the infected fish.

Flukes—Skin and Gill (highly contagious)

Flukes are microscopic parasites that lodge themselves in the gills. The gill fluke *(Dactylogyrus)* is very easily detectable. It causes the gills to swell up pink and red, and the fish spends a lot of time near the surface trying to get air. Sometimes, a puslike fluid will be exuded from the gills. Other symptoms include severe color loss, scratching, and labored respiration. The skin fluke *(Gyrodactylus)* causes localized swelling, excessive mucus, and ulcerations. As with all infestations, weak fish fall victim first.

Like the other parasitic manifestations, the host fish is constantly trying to rub itself against objects to scrape off the infestation. Again, aquarium supply stores have pest-control remedies for this problem, which is more easily treatable than the ones I have already listed. Be sure to treat the tank as well, to make sure this parasite does not spread.

Ich (highly contagious)

Raised white spots about the size of salt granules that appear on the body are the parasite *Ichthyophthirius.* This is one of the most common parasites among aquarium fish. Ich (pronounced *ick*) should not be taken lightly, as it will kill your fish if left untreated.

This ailment is so common that there are many commercial ich remedies on the market. Follow standard instructions and remove the fish and treat it in a hospital tank. The entire aquarium must be treated as well.

Ich manifests as raised white spots. It may be harder to detect on a spotted fish like this Angel.

Velvet (highly contagious)

The parasite *Oodinium* causes a golden velvety coat on the body and fins that is referred to as velvet. In orange fish, such as Goldfish, velvet can be difficult to detect at first. Commercially produced remedies are best for this parasitic affliction. Some experts use the old-fashioned ten-day salt bath. Use a commercial product, but if one is not available try the salt bath. You should add some kind of antifungal chemical to the water of the aquarium to disinfect the tank as well.

Hole-in-the-Head Disease (contagious)

This disease is caused by the parasite *Hexamita,* which is an internal parasite that is harmful when the fish is weakened by stress, age, or poor water quality. It is generally characterized by white, stringy feces and enlarged, pus-filled sensory pores in the head. Other symptoms include erosion of the skin and muscles that eventually extends to the bones and skull. The lateral line is also a common site for these lesions.

Sometimes transferring the fish to larger tanks and implementing frequent water changes are enough to cure the fish. Improved nutrition, supplemented with vitamin C, has been known to improve the condition as well.

Fish Diseases and the Signs and Symptoms

Disease	Signs and Symptoms
Anchor worm	A white worm protrudes from a red, agitated area on the fish's body. Infested fish rubs against anything it can, attempting to scratch off the parasite.
Body slime fungus	Protective skin mucus grows white and starts peeling off, as if the fish were shedding or molting. Fins are eventually covered as well.
China disease	Tail fins and other fins begin to fray, beginning at the base of the fin and working its way outward. Infected areas begin to blacken. Ventral region begins to turn black.
Constipation, indigestion	Fish is very inactive, usually rests on bottom of the tank. Abdominal swelling and bulging is likely.
Dropsy (kidney bloat)	Abdomen bloats noticeably. Scales stick out like pinecones.
Fin or tail rot	Fins have missing parts and eventually become shredded. Rays become inflamed and entire fin may be eaten away.
Fish lice	Round, disk-shaped, transparent crustaceans that clamp onto fish and refuse to let go. Infected fish will rub against objects in the tank in an effort to remove the parasites.
Fish pox	Whitish or pinkish waxy film develops over fish's skin and fins.
Fungus	Fuzzy growth, different from velvet because it is more whitish.
Furunculosis	Raised bumps under the scales that eventually rupture and cause bleeding ulcers.

Disease	Signs and Symptoms
Gill fluke	Gills swell pink and red.
	Fish spends time at the surface gasping for air.
	Puslike fluid will be exuded from the gills.
Hole-in-the-head	Fish has white, stringy feces and enlarged pus-filled sensory pores in the head.
	Also, erosion of the skin and muscles that eventually extends to the bones and skull.
Ich	Raised white spots about the size of a salt granule appear on the body and fins.
Leeches	Long, wormlike parasites attached at both ends to the fish that do not come off easily.
Mouth fungus	White cottony growth on mouth, sometimes spreading to the gills and other parts.
Pop-eye	Fish's eyes protrude from an inflamed eye socket.
Skin fluke	Localized swelling, excessive mucus and ulcerations on skin.
	The fish is constantly trying to rid itself of these parasites by rubbing against aquarium objects.
Swim bladder disease	Fish swims on its side, upside down, or somersaults through the water.
	Fish may be found either on the top or the bottom of the tank.
Tumors	Obvious bumps, lumps, and protrusions that sometimes look like large blisters or warts.
Ulcers	Large red lesions, boils, dark reddening, and bleeding.
Velvet	Fuzzy yellow or golden areas.

Chapter 9

Breeding Your Freshwater Fish

As you become more involved in your aquarium and as you gain experience in how to maintain a healthy habitat for your pets, you may want to get into fish breeding. This can be as simple as letting your guppies give birth to their young in your tank, or as complex as setting up a special breeding aquarium for mouthbrooding Cichlids. Serious fish breeders ultimately take the latter route if they intend to produce young that will survive.

Fish breeding is a vast and complex topic that has been covered in a wide variety of books. This chapter presents the basics of fish reproduction, spawning behavior, and breeding techniques. Before you set out to seriously breed your fish, I recommend that you consult some of the references listed in the appendix for a more complete understanding of this topic.

Natural Reproduction

Fish have evolved different modes of reproduction that are directly related to the habitat in which they live. For example, fish in the open ocean tend to broadcast large numbers of eggs and sperm into the water column, where they develop in the plankton never to be seen by their parents. On the opposite end of the spectrum are lake and river fish, for which numerous hiding places allow for nest building and parental care.

Like other vertebrates, fish require both males and females to produce offspring. In fish, the gonads, organs that produce eggs (ovaries) and sperm (testes), lie inside the abdominal cavity. For this reason, it is not always easy to tell the sexes apart, with the exception of the livebearing fish.

Natural reproduction in fish is usually stimulated by a variety of biological and environmental conditions. In temperate areas where there are seasonal changes, fish have a tendency to reproduce in the spring and summer when the temperature is highest, the days are longest, and food is plentiful. In tropical areas, fish reproduce year-round because these factors do not change greatly.

For most freshwater tropical fish, temperature is not a major factor, but seasonal changes in rainfall, day length, and water chemistry usually trigger breeding several times a year. If you intend to become a serious fish breeder, you need to mimic the natural conditions that stimulate fish breeding.

In the natural environment, predation among fish is a common part of the reproductive cycle. Whether a livebearing or egglaying species, young fish are expected to leave the nest at some point—or be eaten. For livebearing fish, this generally occurs right after birth. For egglaying species, the young may be protected until they reach a certain size and move away.

If a young fish moves into an area inhabited by an adult fish, the adult will assume the young fish is not her own and is likely to eat it. Actually, this strategy has evolved to ensure survival of her offspring. Similarly, weak or sickly young who stay close to their mother are likely to be consumed. This leads to a greater energy supply for the next brood and ensures survival of the species. A drastic change in environmental conditions also causes a parent to eat its young to survive.

Angelfish deposit their eggs on flat surfaces and on vegetation.

Reproduction in the Aquarium

There are many factors that must be considered in a home aquarium when you decide to breed your fish. Remember, you are trying to mimic the natural environment of fish.

First, take into account the fish's reproductive mode (livebearer or egglayer). Then consider the environmental conditions that initiate breeding and maximize survival of the young. Finally, know when the adult is most likely to consume its young and separate them accordingly. Even if there is some parental care, at some point the parents expect their young to leave the nest or they will be consumed.

Next, you must select high-quality parent stock. The primary objective of breeding your fish is to produce viable, healthy offspring, so start with excellent parent fish. Those chosen for breeding should be healthy, energetic fish with flawless form, coloration, and fins. In most cases, it is best if the parents are not related, since indiscriminate inbreeding results in inferior offspring. There are exceptions to this when you are trying to perfect a certain variety or strain of fish, such as Goldfish or Guppies.

Some experts recommend that you cull inferior offspring as well. This depends on your breeding objectives. If you are going to be raising your fry for sale or for further breeding, don't waste the time and energy raising inferior fish. Remove deformed or undersized offspring and feed them to other fish.

The Breeding Tank

While many species of aquarium fish, particularly the livebearers, will breed right in your community aquarium, the serious breeder should set up a spawning or breeding tank. This small aquarium enables you to establish special tank conditions that trigger spawning. It also isolates the parents and the fry so that they can be closely monitored, and increases the survival of the young fish. In addition, some species of fish, such as Cichlids, become extremely aggressive and territorial during the spawning period. Moving these fish to a breeding tank spares your other fish the grief associated with this behavior.

The breeding tank should be set up according to the type of fish you intend to breed. Tank size, gravel, plants, decorations, heating, and filtration requirements vary with species. In general, the types of plants and gravel depend on whether the fish is a livebearer or an egglayer. In most cases, filtration should be kept simple. Large power filters suck delicate fry to certain death. A box filter or a small power filter with fine screening over the intakes will suffice in the breeding tank. As in the main aquarium, aeration should be provided.

Cichlids, like this Feiberg's Peacock, become very aggressive and territorial while spawning.

Livebearers

As the name implies, livebearers give birth to living young. The scientific term for this is "viviparous." In viviparous species of fish, males and females mate and the sperm is transferred to the female via specialized pelvic fins called gonopodia in most fish (or claspers in sharks). The eggs are fertilized internally and development within the female requires days, weeks, or months, depending on the species. The female then gives birth to fry at an advanced stage of development and the young do not require a lot of parental care.

A livebearing female can produce multiple broods from one mating because she is able to store sperm in her body for several months. Young can be produced every few weeks and brood sizes can be quite large, up to one hundred fry.

There are more than a dozen families of livebearing fish, and many are sharks and rays. Mollies, Guppies, Swordtails, and Platies are livebearing species that you are likely to have in your first aquarium. The sexes of these fish are readily distinguishable by the presence of a gonopodium on the male. In addition, females tend to be more drab in coloration. Pregnant females are also easily recognizable by their bulging abdomens.

A Tank Divider

The tank divider may seem like an ideal alternative to setting up a breeding tank, but it may create more problems than it solves. A tank divider is simply a piece of plastic with small holes that fits into the aquarium, thereby dividing it into two separate sections. The pregnant female is placed in one section, while the other fish remain in the main section. The divider allows water to pass between sections but not the fry. However, you must have a large enough aquarium space to commit a section to breeding livebearers. Also, tank conditions cannot be modified to meet the requirements of the young and, at the same time, not disrupt the rest of the community. Nonetheless, in a pinch, the tank divider will suffice until a breeding tank can be established.

Livebearers have no problem breeding and giving birth in your community aquarium. However, most or all of the young are likely to be consumed by other fish if a large amount of cover is not provided for the fry. The best way to prevent this from happening is to place the pregnant female into a separate spawning tank or to buy a tank divider (see the box above).

For livebearers, the breeding tank must be heavily vegetated to protect the fry from immediate consumption by the mother. In general, floating plants are ideal for this. Some experts also recommend the use of a spawning trap. This simple device can be purchased at your local aquarium supply store. The spawning trap is a fine-mesh cage that fits into the tank. The pregnant female is then placed into the trap, where she gives birth to her young. The fine mesh allows the fry to pass to safety, while retaining the cannibalistic mother. After the female gives birth, allow her to rest for a couple of days before returning her to the main aquarium. Young fish should be kept isolated from the larger fish until they reach comparable size.

This Painted Platy female is not as brightly colored as her male counterpart.

Egglayers

Egglaying fish are referred to as "oviparous." The vast majority of fish are egglayers. In this reproductive group, fertilization of the eggs occurs outside the female's body. In general, the eggs and sperm are deposited or released into the water, where they are fertilized by the male. The eggs of these species contain large amounts of yolk that sustain development. The embryos develop within the egg for a period of time ranging from days to months, depending on the species.

During this time and immediately after hatching, these fish are extremely susceptible to predation. Therefore, oviparous species generally release very large numbers of eggs to ensure the survival of at least a few of their young. There is also a tendency among these fish to protect and care for their eggs and fry to increase survival.

This group of fish can be further classified based on how they deposit or release their eggs. This determines how you set up your breeding tank. I have divided the egglayers into five groups: egg scatterers, egg depositors, egg buriers, nest builders, and mouthbrooders.

Egg Scatterers

Egg scatterers, as the name implies, broadcast eggs and milt (sperm) all over the aquarium. These fish usually spawn in schools or pairs. After mixing with milt in the water column, the fertilized eggs float in the current or fall to the bottom among the gravel and stones, where they remain unguarded. Unfortunately, this is the most difficult group to breed because the unguarded eggs are rapidly consumed by the parents as well as other occupants of the aquarium. Common egg scatterers include Characins, such as the Cardinal Tetra and some of the Barbs.

To effectively breed egg scatterers, condition the sexes separately before placing them together in the spawning tank. Check the special water quality requirements of the species you intend to spawn and mimic these in your spawning tank. For example, Cardinal Tetras require some change in water chemistry to initiate spawning—in this case, slightly acidic pH and softer water.

The breeding tank for the egg scatterer should be modified to reduce egg eating by the parents. This can be done in a number of ways. You can cover the bottom of the tank with glass marbles so that eggs fall between them and cannot be eaten. Feathery plants also provide suitable substrate for these fish while protecting the eggs. Some aquarists prefer to drape a piece of fine-mesh netting in the water. The spawning fish are placed above the netting, and the eggs fall through the mesh and away from the mouths of the parents. In all cases, the parents should be removed from the breeding tank after spawning.

Red Rasboras are among the fish that lay eggs.

Axelrod's Corydoras is an egg depositor.

Egg Depositors

Egg depositors lay their eggs on flat surfaces or in vegetation. Flat rocks and fine-leafed plants are ideal spawning substrate for these species. After deposition by the female, the eggs are fertilized by the male. In most cases, egg depositors guard their eggs and fry. This group includes some of the Cichlids, such as the Angelfish, Killifish, Rainbowfish, as well as Catfish, such as the Corydoras.

The breeding tank for egg depositors varies with species. Fine-leafed plants or spawning mops provide suitable substrate for Killifish and Rainbowfish. Flat rocks, broad-leafed plants, and clean, empty flowerpots should dominate the breeding tank of the Cichlids and Catfish. Some aquarists move the rock or spawning mop with the attached eggs to another tank for hatching.

Egg Buriers

Egg buriers lay their eggs and bury them in the soft substrate. Killifish are the most well-known of the egg buriers. The best way to accommodate these fish is to provide suitable soft substrate, such as peat, so they can bury their eggs.

An African Jewel Cichlid with his fry. A fishkeeper needs to be aware of the point at which the fry and parents must be separated.

Nest Builders

Nest builders include many species of fish that dig depressions in the substrate and deposit their eggs in a nest. Many Cichlid species build nests, which they defend. Gouramis build another kind of nest, called a bubblenest. Males construct this nest by expelling air from the mouth. In the case of the Siamese Fighting Fish, the female releases her eggs and the male deposits them into the bubblenest. The eggs hatch within forty-eight hours and the male tends the nest and the fry for up to ten days. He should be removed at this time, before he eats the fry.

The breeding tank of the nest builders does not require many special adaptations. Most of the problems with nest building Cichlids are associated with the pairing of mates. These fish tend to be aggressive and choosy about their mates. It is recommended that several juveniles are kept together to allow natural pairing. The pair should then be transferred to a breeding tank by themselves for courtship and spawning.

Bubblenest builders require no special breeding setup in the spawning tank. In some species, such as the Siamese Fighting Fish, the male is very aggressive and the sexes must be kept separate until spawning time. A tank divider keeps the sexes apart until they are ready for spawning. Females should be removed after spawning, while the male tends to the eggs and fry.

Mouthbrooders

Mouthbrooders actually hold the eggs and fry in their mouths for days or weeks, depending on the species. This is a very high level of parental care that results in the successful rearing of well-developed fry. The most popular species of mouthbrooders are the African Lake Cichlids.

In some cases, both sexes participate in the parental care while, in others, only the female broods the eggs. In general, a female deposits eggs on a flat surface then picks them up into her oral cavity, where they are held until they hatch. Fertilization occurs either on the flat surface or in the female's mouth. After hatching, the fry may continue to seek shelter in her mouth.

The breeding tank of the mouthbrooder does not require any special setup, other than a flat surface for initial egg deposition. There are, however, special water quality considerations that must be maintained when trying to breed species such as African Lake Cichlids. Check some of the books listed in the appendix for information on feeding and raising fry.

This Lombardo's Cichlid is native to Lake Malawi in Africa, and is a mouthbrooder.

Learning More About Your Freshwater Aquarium

There are millions of home aquarists all over the world. As you become more involved in aquarium keeping, you will be surprised at how many people share this avocation. I found myself going to my local aquarium supply dealer just to see new fish arrivals, talk about aquarium problems, and exchange ideas with fellow aquarists. I have picked up some of the most valuable information on fishkeeping from amateurs who enjoy the thrills and delights of fishkeeping.

Clubs

In many areas, aquarium enthusiasts have established clubs and associations where ideas and techniques are endlessly bantered about. You will find these organizations by asking your local aquarium supply dealer. Not only are these kinds of organizations great for gathering information, but they also help you find and buy used equipment as well as healthy homebred fish.

Magazines

Monthly aquarium magazines provide you with some of the most up-to-date information on aquarium keeping. Timely articles on breeding, feeding, disease, and species-specific husbandry will both entertain and inform. In addition, product information and classified advertising are excellent, useful features. The photos are pretty cool, as well.

The most popular magazines that have proven to be very good conduits of information include:

Aquarium Fish Magazine
P.O. Box 6050
Mission Viejo, CA 92690-6050
(949) 855-8822
www.aquariumfish.com

Freshwater and Marine Aquarium
P.O. Box 487
Sierra Madre, CA 91025
(800) 523-1736
www.famamagazine.com

Marine Fish Monthly
3243 Highway 61
East Luttrell, TN 37779
(800) 937-3963

Practical Fishkeeping
EMAP Apex
Apex House, Oundle Road
Peterborough, PE2 9NP, UK
01733 898100
www.practicalfishkeeping.co.uk

Tropical Fish Hobbyist
One TFH Plaza
Neptune City, NJ 07753
(908) 988-8400

Fish on the Internet

If you have access to the Internet, then you have unlimited access to a vast amount of information on this hobby. Internet resources include chat groups, equipment, photos, links, husbandry information, classified ads, events, and on and on and on. Some Internet access companies have even established networks for fish enthusiasts that you can join. Membership in a network gives you access to hobbyists, professional aquarists, researchers, breeders, and vendors of aquarium products. You can also get immediate advice from staff experts about sick fish.

There is so much on the Internet that you will quickly be overwhelmed with all the options. Don't forget that many experts and vendors have home pages as well. Any good search engine will help you access these resources, but here are a few sites that I like.

- Aqua Link, www.aqualink.com
- Aquaria Central, www.aquariacentral.com
- Aquarium.net, www.aquarium.net
- Aquatic Book Shop, www.seahorses.com

- Fish Base, www.fishbase.org
- Fish Index. www.fishindex.com
- Fish Info Service, info-s.com/fish.html
- Fish Link Central, www.fishlinkcentral.com
- Reef Aquarium Farming News, www.garf.org/news.html
- Sea and Sky, www.seasky.org/sea.html

Books

Literally thousands of books have been published on every facet of aquarium keeping. The list below is a mere smattering of what is available for the new and experienced aquarist. Each one of those books has its own bibliography, which will help you delve further into the field.

Axelrod, H.R., *Encyclopedia of Tropical Fishes: With Special Emphasis on Techniques of Breeding,* TFH Publications, 1986.

Axelrod, H. R. and L. P. Schultz, *Handbook of Tropical Aquarium Fishes,* TFH Publications, 1990.

Bailey, M. and P. Burgess, *Tropical Fishlopaedia,* Howell Book House, 2000.

Bailey, M. and G. Sandford, *The Ultimate Aquarium,* Smithmark Publishers, 1995.

Burgess P., M. Bailey, and A. Exell, *A-Z of Tropical Fish Diseases and Health Problems,* Howell Book House, 1999.

Gratzek, J. B., *Aquariology: Fish Diseases and Water Chemistry,* Tetra Press, 1992.

Halstead, B. W. and B. L. Landa, *Tropical Fish,* Golden Press, 1985.

Hargrove, M. and M. Hargrove, *Aquariums For Dummies,* Wiley Publishing, Inc., 1999.

Helfman, G. S., B. B. Collette, and D. E. Facey, *The Diversity of Fishes,* Blackwell Science, 1999.

Hiscock, P., *Creating a Natural Aquarium,* Howell Book House, 2000.

James, B. A., *Fishkeeper's Guide to Aquarium Plants,* Salamander Books, 1986.

Mills, D., *Understanding Freshwater Fish,* Howell Book House, 2000.

Sandford, G., *An Illustrated Encyclopedia of Aquarium Fish,* Howell Book House, 1995.

Sandford, G., *Understanding Tropical Fish,* Howell Book House, 2000.

Scheurmann, I., *Water Plants in the Aquarium,* Barron's, 1987.

Scott, P. W., *The Complete Aquarium,* Dorling Kindersley Publishing, 1995.

Stoskopf, M. K., *Fish Medicine,* W. B. Saunders Co., 1993.

Stratton, R. F., *Aquarium Filtration,* Yearbooks, Inc., 2000.

Index